grilling

a dierbergs school of cooking publication

Dierbergs

Grilling
A Dierbergs School of Cooking Publication

Copyright 2008
Dierbergs Markets, Inc.
16690 Swingley Ridge Road
Chesterfield, Missouri 63017

This cookbook is a collection of recipes, which has been developed and tested by Dierbergs Home Economists.

All rights reserved. No part of this publication may be reproduced in any form or by any means, electronic or mechanical, including photocopy and information storage and retrieval systems, without permission in writing from the publisher.

ISBN: 978-0-9749955-4-0
First Printing 2008

*Cover photograph:
Whiskey Pepper Chops
with Molasses Butter
Recipe on page 37*

Acknowledgements

Director of Marketing and Advertising
John Muckerman

Managing Editor
Gena Bast

Food Editor
Barb Ridenhour

Cookbook Project Manager
Janice Martin

Copywriters
Gena Bast, Therese Lewis

Art Director/Designer
Mike Parker

Dierbergs School of Cooking Managers
Sally Bruns, Loretta Evans, Ginger Gall, Jennifer Kassel, Nancy Lorenz

Photography
Steve Adams, Steve Adams Studio

Food Stylists
Carol Ziemann
Linda Behrends (pages 66 and 80)

Food Styling Assistant
Janice Martin

Prop Stylist, Dierbergs Test Kitchen Manager
Karen Hurych

Nutrition Analysis
Trish Farano, D.T.R., Dierbergs Markets
Sherri Hoyt, R.D., Missouri Baptist Medical Center

Recipe Editing
Patty Tomaselli

Contributors
Cathy Chipley, Chef Jack West MacMurray III, Pam Pahl, Carol Ziemann

TABLE OF contents

Introduction	5
Grilling Basics	7
SAUCES, RUBS & MORE	10
BEEF & PORK	18
POULTRY, FISH & SEAFOOD	40
SIDES & MEATLESS	60
DESSERTS	82
Nutrition Information	91
Equivalents	92
Food Safety	92
How Much Meat Should I Buy	92
Dierbergs School of Cooking	93
Index	94

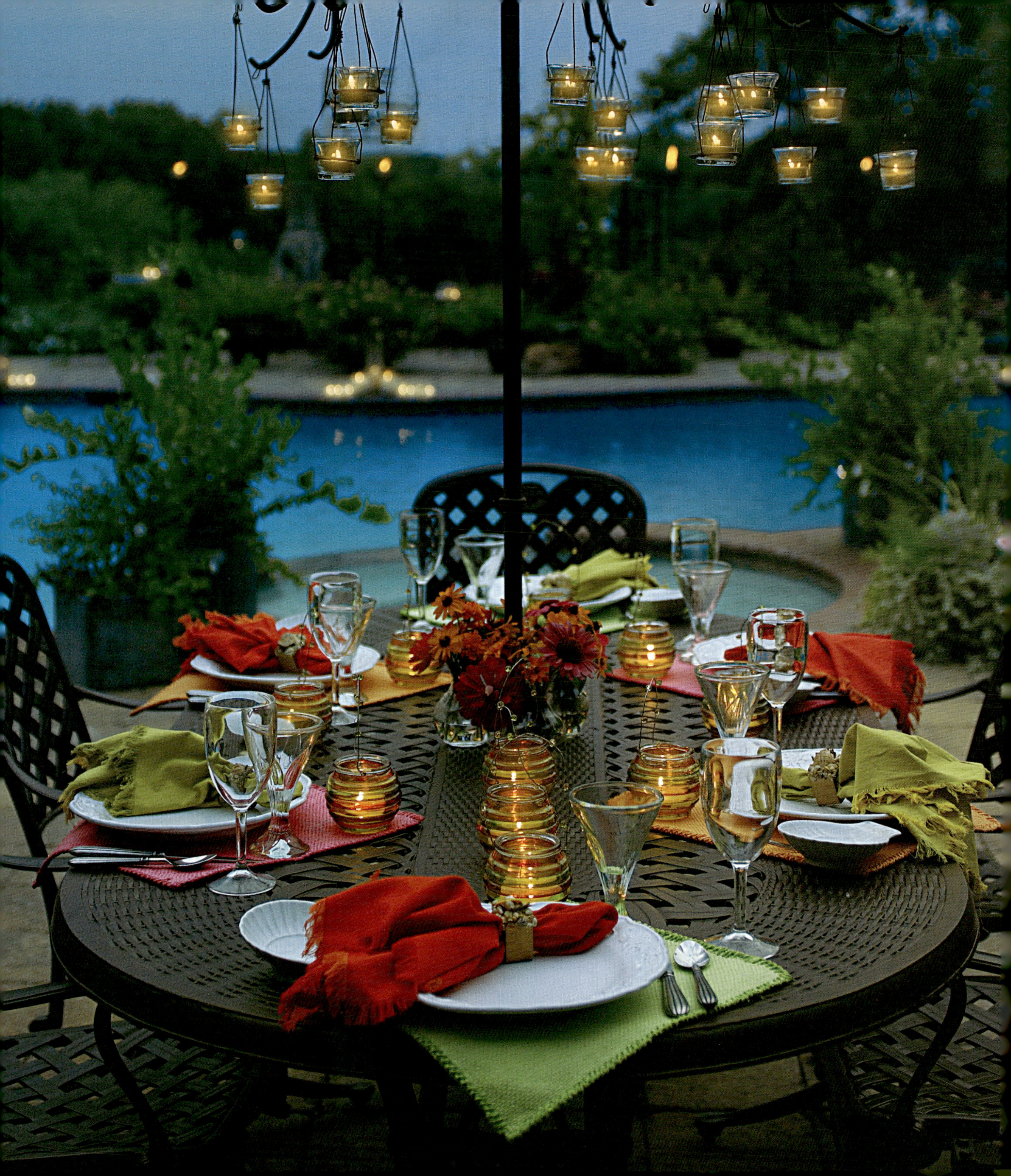

Introduction

There's nothing quite so inviting as the aroma and sounds of an outdoor sizzling feast in progress. Whether it's as simple as grilled burgers for a backyard barbecue or thick, juicy steaks for a patio dinner party, the results are a memorable meal every time.

Grilling is timeless and one of the most universal cooking methods enjoyed by many cultures. It isn't complicated. You don't need fancy equipment. Whether you prefer charcoal or gas . . . choose to marinate, rub or sauce . . . the mouth-watering flavors are always bold, fun and deliciously smoky.

Ready to step up to the grill? This comprehensive collection of sure-fire recipes from Dierbergs School of Cooking will have you grilling with confidence. Try Chicago-Style Steaks with Blue Cheese Butter (page 20) or Tropical Spiced Chicken with Ginger Peach Salsa (page 44) or Summer Vegetables with Bowtie Pasta (page 77). Spice things up with our Southwest Potato Salad (page 65). And for dessert, our Berry Peachy Cobbler (page 87) is a piece of cake!

The thrill of the grill. We hope you will be inspired to serve these recipes to your family and friends.

GREG'S GRILLING TIP

Greg Dierberg spends many an evening at the grill where he enjoys cooking for family and friends. Look for his expert tips and suggestions throughout this cookbook.

You'll find the *Eat Hearty* logo, indicating foods meeting heart-healthy criteria, on more than half of the entrées (see more information on page 91).

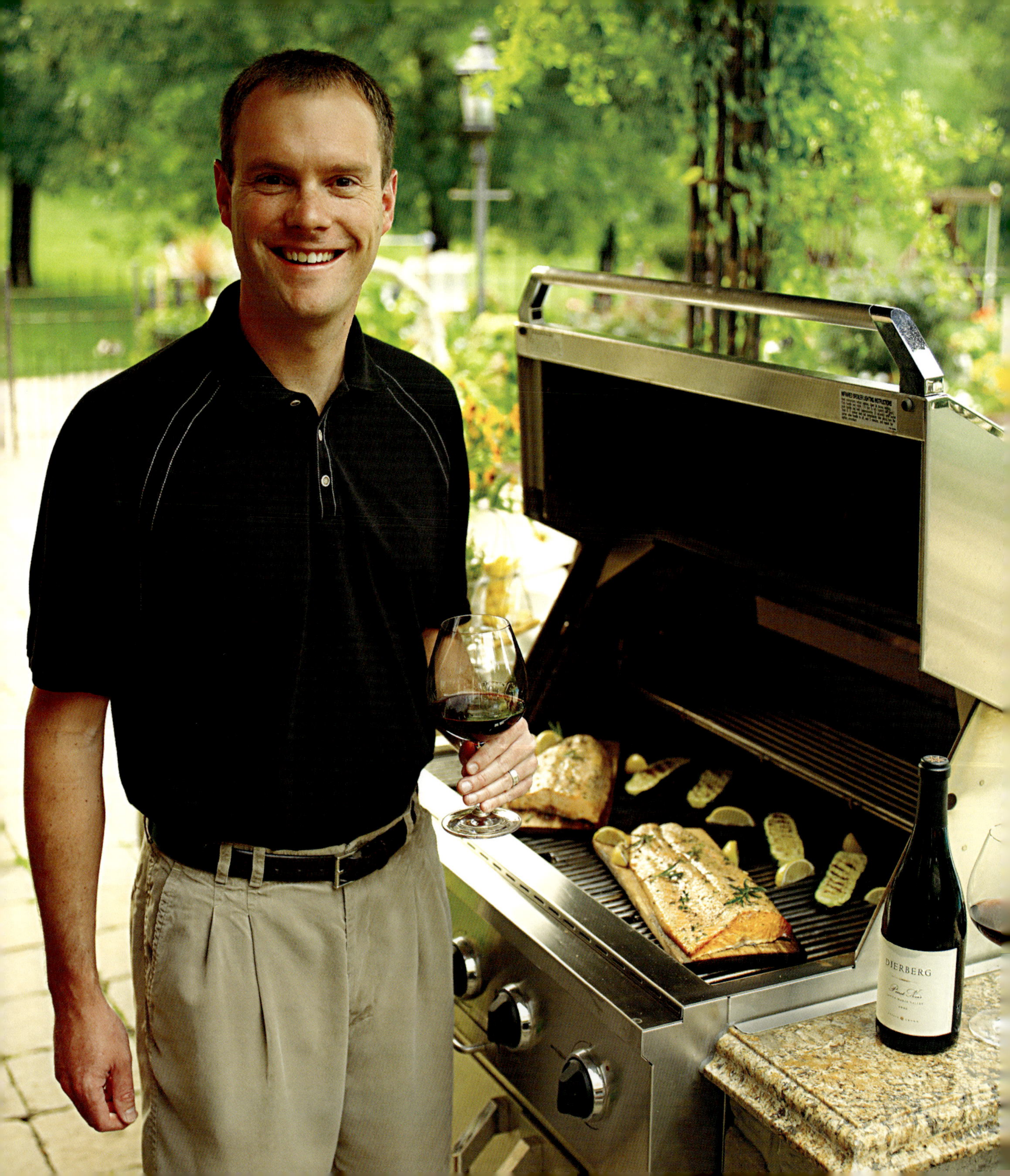
DJERBERG

Grilling Basics

Direct or Indirect?

Just like cooking indoors, the "one-size-fits-all" approach doesn't apply to grilling. Here are some tips for cooking with gas or charcoal over direct or indirect heat.

Direct-Heat Grilling

This method is ideal for foods that take less than 30 minutes to cook, like steaks, chops, kabobs, and burgers. Place food directly over the burners or coals, turning once during cooking. Sear large cuts of meat over direct heat, and then finish grilling over indirect heat.

FOR GAS GRILLS For proper browning and quick cooking of foods, always preheat the grill for at least 15 minutes with the lid down and all burners on high. Adjust burners according to recipe directions before placing food on grid.

FOR CHARCOAL GRILLS Use a charcoal chimney to light the coals quickly. This eliminates the need for lighter fluid, which can add an off-flavor to foods. Follow manufacturer's directions for starting the fire, and let it burn for about 15 minutes until all coals are glowing. Wear an oven mitt and pour out the coals into an even mound. Wait until the coals are ash-covered, about 10 minutes, before placing food on grid.

Indirect-Heat Grilling

This method allows food to cook more slowly, more like oven roasting. Use indirect heat for large cuts of meat like roasts, whole chicken, turkey, and ribs.

FOR GAS GRILLS Preheat the grill for about 15 minutes with the lid down and all burners on high. Turn off the burners in the center or on one side where the food will sit. Turn the remaining burners to medium or low according to recipe directions. Meat can be placed on a rack over a disposable foil pan to catch drippings. Cover the grill and cook until done, lifting the lid as little as possible to maintain heat. Slide a baking sheet under the foil pan before removing it from the grill.

FOR CHARCOAL GRILLS Use a charcoal chimney to light the coals (see Direct-Heat Grilling for Charcoal Grills above). When the coals are ash-covered, place a foil pan in the center to catch fat and juices that drip, and arrange the coals around it. Place the food on the grid above the drip pan. Cover the grill and cook until done, lifting the lid as little as possible and adding charcoal to the sides of the fire as needed to maintain steady heat.

◀ *Greg Dierberg*

Plank Cooking

Grilling food on planks is flavorful, delicious, and best of all – easy. Just follow the directions on the plank package and these tips for tasty results.

- Use planks that are designed specifically for cooking, not lumber from the hardware store. Resinous woods like pine, poplar, and birch will impart an unpleasant flavor.

- Use planks for outdoor cooking only. Soak the plank, and preheat it for about 3 minutes before adding food.

- Place food directly on the plank and close the lid. Don't peek! You lose heat each time you lift the lid, which prolongs the cooking time.

- Planks may be used a second time if they are not too charred. Wash and rinse them thoroughly, and let dry. Break heavily charred planks into chunks to use as wood chips in your grill.

Controlling Charcoal Heat

Hold your hand over the coals at grid height (about 5 inches above the fire) to estimate how hot the fire is.

The fire is:	If you can hold your hand in place for:
Hot	2 seconds or less and coals are glowing brightly
Medium-hot	3 to 4 seconds and coals are glowing brightly with faint coating of ash
Medium	5 to 6 seconds and coals are glowing with light coating of ash
Low	7 seconds or more and coals are barely glowing with thick coating of ash

Grill Safety

Place the grill on a level surface in an open area. Make sure it's clear of any enclosures, overhangs, or combustible items.

Use fire starters that are specifically designed for grill use. Be sure to store them in a secure place away from any heat source. Never spray flammable liquids on already-lit charcoal.

Use a charcoal chimney or electric-coil starter on charcoal grills, but never on gas grills.

After removing lit coals from a chimney starter, place the chimney on a fireproof surface away from anyone who might touch it and well clear of anything flammable.

Keep children and pets away from a hot grill, and never leave it unattended.

Keep a water spray bottle handy to control flare-ups, or just cover the grill until flames subside. You can also move food to a cooler side of the grid.

Minimum Safe Internal Temperatures

Use an instant-read or meat thermometer to determine the internal temperature of foods. Follow individual recipes for optimal end temperatures. Use the following chart as a guide for minimum safe temperatures.

Beef, medium-rare	145°F.
Beef, ground	160°F.
Fish	145°F.
Pork, chops or tenderloin	160°F.
Pork, roast	150°F.
Pork, ground or sausage	155°F.
Poultry	165°F.
Casseroles	165°F.
Previously cooked foods	165°F.

Is It Done?

When it comes to determining the doneness of meat, fish, and poultry, looks alone can be deceiving. Smoked foods often look pink when they are done. Here are some helpful hints for delicious results every time.

Thermometers

Using a thermometer is the most accurate way to determine whether food is done. Insert the thermometer into the center of the meat. Avoid touching fat, bone, or stuffing. Taking the temperature of thinner cuts of meat can be tricky. Thermometers inserted from the top may go all the way through the meat. For an accurate reading, insert the thermometer about one inch into the side of the meat rather than through the top.

Meat thermometers have large dials that indicate the temperature and sometimes have a scale that describes the doneness (rare, medium, well). They are oven-safe and designed to be inserted in the food at the beginning of the cooking time and left in while it cooks.

Instant-read thermometers take a food's temperature in seconds. They have smaller dials and are inserted in food near the end of cooking time just long enough to check the temperature. These thermometers are not oven-safe.

Standing Time

Stop! Put down that knife and let the meat rest before slicing. Juices rise to the surface during cooking and need a few minutes to settle back into the meat.

When the meat is done, tent it loosely with foil and let the meat rest. About 5 to 10 minutes is perfect for steaks and pork tenderloin, and about 15 to 20 minutes for large roasts, whole chickens, or turkeys.

Proper standing time makes meats easier to carve into neat slices, and each bite will be tender and juicy.

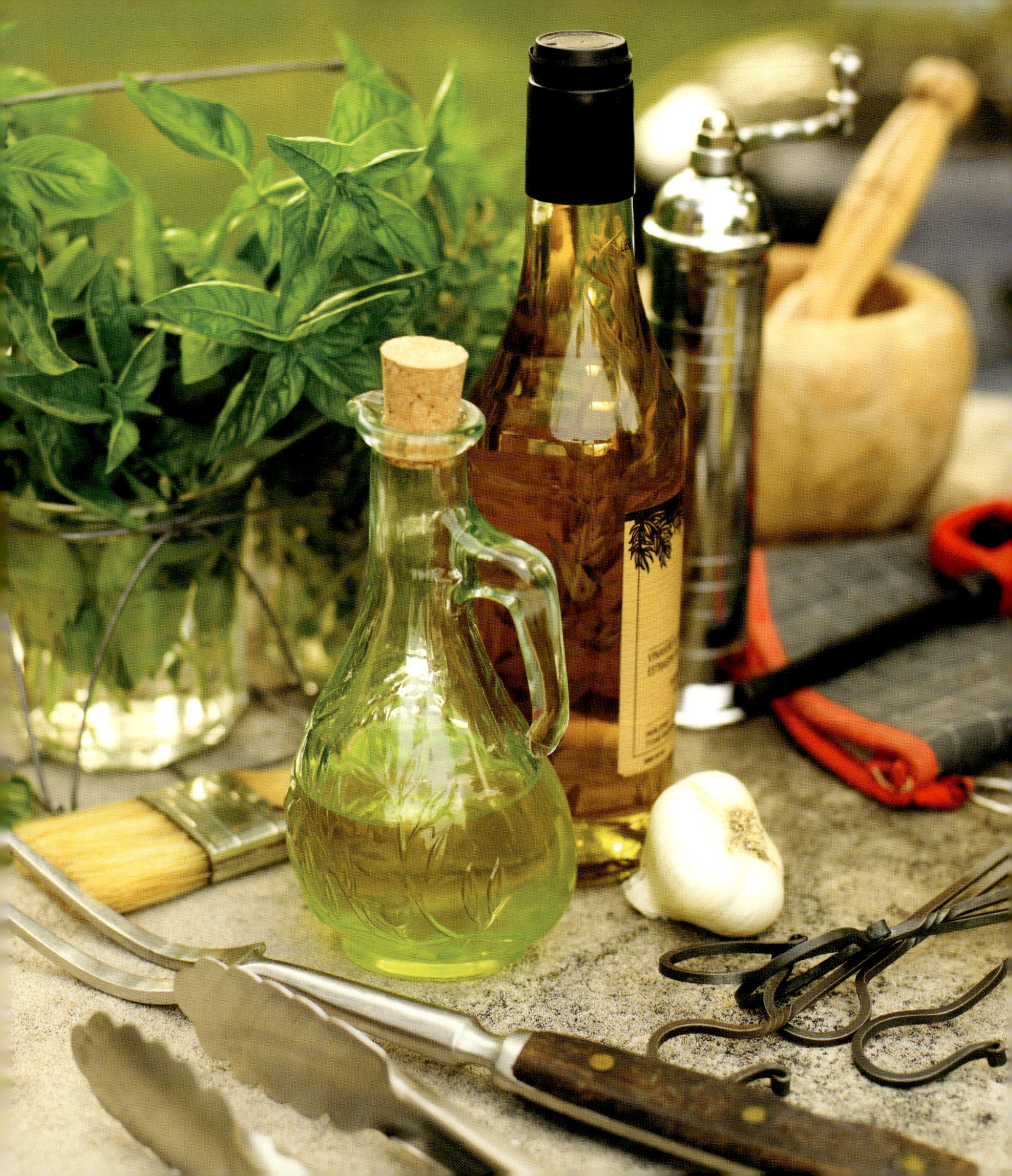

sauces, rubs & more

Best-Ever Barbecue Sauce	12
Chili Cherry Sauce	12
Raspberry Balsamic Glaze	13
Pickapeppa Glaze	13
Caribbean Glaze	13
Balsamic Marinade	14
Ginger Marinade	14
Mojo Marinade	14
Red Wine Marinade	15
Tandoori Marinade	15
Tuscan Marinade	15
Basic Brine	16
Beer Brine	16
Java Brine	16
Fresh Herb Rub	17
Island Rub	17
Southwest Rub	17

SAUCES

Best-Ever Barbecue Sauce

Forget bottled sauce. This one is everything you love – sweet, spicy, tangy, and delicious. You'll love it on our Sweet and Spicy Pork Steaks and Spareribs (recipes on page 30).

technique savvy

Bring on the Sauce

No doubt in America that there's hardly a drumstick or sparerib on a backyard grill that isn't slathered with some kind of barbecue sauce. Whether we buy it in a bottle or cook up our *secret recipe*, we can't get enough of the sweet, sticky stuff. But let the barbecuer beware – sauce burns easily because of the high sugar content. To improve the odds of deliciously glazed food without a charred exterior, brush sauce on only during the last 10 minutes of cooking time.

2 cups ketchup
1/2 cup beer or apple juice
1/2 cup strong brewed coffee
1/2 cup honey
2 tablespoons Worcestershire sauce
2 teaspoons chili powder
1 teaspoon ground cumin
Salt and pepper to taste

In medium saucepan, combine all ingredients over medium-high heat; bring to a boil. Reduce heat, cover, and simmer until slightly thickened, about 10 minutes. Store in refrigerator.

Makes 3 1/2 cups

Per 2 tablespoons Calories 39; Fat 0 g; Cholesterol 0 mg; Sodium 207 mg; Carbohydrate 10 g; Fiber <1 g

Chili Cherry Sauce

This sweet and sassy cherry sauce is terrific on pork. Try our recipe for Chili Cherry Chops (page 38) and Chili Cherry Pork Kabobs (page 26).

1 jar (10 to 12 ounces) cherry preserves
1 cup chopped onion
1/2 cup chili sauce
1/4 cup firmly packed brown sugar
2 cloves garlic, minced
1/2 teaspoon ground red pepper
1 tablespoon dark sesame oil (optional)

In medium saucepan, combine all ingredients except sesame oil over medium-high heat; bring to a boil. Reduce heat and simmer for 20 minutes. Cool to room temperature. Stir in sesame oil. Store in refrigerator.

Makes 2 cups

Per 2 tablespoons Calories 85; Fat 1 g; Cholesterol 0 mg; Sodium 248 mg; Carbohydrate 19 g; Fiber <1 g

GLAZES

Raspberry Balsamic Glaze

This easy sweet and sour glaze is perfect for chicken and pork. Also try apple jelly with cider vinegar; peach preserves with raspberry vinegar; and orange marmalade with white balsamic vinegar.

1/2 cup seedless raspberry jam, melted
1 tablespoon balsamic vinegar

In 1-cup glass measure, stir together jam and vinegar. Store in refrigerator.

Makes 1/2 cup

Per 2 tablespoons Calories 116; Fat 0 g; Cholesterol 0 mg; Sodium 14 mg; Carbohydrate 29 g; Fiber <1 g

Pickapeppa Glaze

Pickapeppa sauce, found in the condiment aisle, makes a lively Jamaican glaze for Pickapeppa Beef Kabobs (page 26) or Tropical Spiced Chicken (page 44).

1/4 cup Pickapeppa sauce
2 cloves garlic, minced
1 tablespoon honey
1 teaspoon jerk seasoning
1 teaspoon brown sugar

In 1-cup glass measure, stir together all ingredients. Store in refrigerator.

Makes about 1/4 cup

Per 2 tablespoons Calories 13; Fat 0 g; Cholesterol 0 mg; Sodium 381 mg; Carbohydrate 9 g; Fiber <1 g

Caribbean Glaze

This sweet and tangy glaze has been one of our favorites for years. Brush it on chicken or pork during the last 10 minutes of grilling. You'll love Caribbean Chicken Kabobs (page 26)!

1 jar (9 ounces) Major Grey's chutney
1/2 cup firmly packed brown sugar
1/4 cup stone ground mustard
1/4 cup dark rum

In work bowl of food processor fitted with steel knife blade or in blender container, combine all ingredients. Process until smooth. In small saucepan, heat sauce mixture over medium-high heat until boiling. Remove from heat; reserve about half to serve as sauce. Store in refrigerator.

Makes 1 1/2 cups

Per 2 tablespoons Calories 117; Fat 0 g; Cholesterol 0 mg; Sodium 254 mg; Carbohydrate 25 g; Fiber 0 g

---

technique savvy

Safety First

Don't let your backyard barbecue plans go up in flames. Keep these simple tips in mind for an outdoor feast that's fun for everyone:

• Set up the grill on solid, level ground and don't leave the fire unattended, especially when children are around.

• Roll up sleeves, secure loose-fitting clothing, and tie back long hair before you start the fire.

• For charcoal grills, use starters designed for grilling, not kerosene or gasoline, and store them safely away from the barbecue site.

MARINADES

Balsamic Marinade

Balsamic Grilled Sirloin (page 24) gets a blast of flavor from this herb marinade. Try it on chicken or pork, too.

1/4 cup olive oil
1/4 cup balsamic vinegar
1/4 cup snipped fresh parsley
2 tablespoons snipped fresh thyme
2 cloves garlic, minced

In 1-cup glass measure, stir together all ingredients.

Makes about 3/4 cup

Ginger Marinade

This Asian-style marinade adds terrific flavor to Gingered Shrimp Salad (page 53). It also pairs well with beef or pork.

1/3 cup rice or white wine vinegar
1/3 cup soy sauce
1 tablespoon dark sesame oil
2 tablespoons minced fresh ginger root
1 clove garlic, minced

In 1-cup glass measure, whisk together all ingredients.

Makes about 3/4 cup

Mojo Marinade

Mojo (MOH-ho), a classic Latin blend, adds pizzazz to Mojo Shrimp Salad (page 53). It's a great way to flavor beef, chicken, or pork, too.

1/3 cup orange juice concentrate, thawed (undiluted)
1/3 cup fresh lime juice
2 cloves garlic, minced
1 tablespoon snipped fresh cilantro or Italian parsley
1 teaspoon chipotle purée (see sidebar on page 21)
1/2 teaspoon salt
1/4 cup olive oil

In 2-cup glass measure, whisk together all ingredients except olive oil. Whisking vigorously, add olive oil in slow, steady stream until well blended.

Makes about 1 cup

---

technique savvy

Safe Marinating Is No Accident

Marinades not only give foods great flavor, they go a long way in tenderizing meat. Acidic ingredients, like vinegar, soy sauce, beer, wine, and fruit juice, break down tough proteins and connective tissues.

Tender cuts of meat – tender steaks, tenderloins, chicken, and fish – should marinate for a short time. Meats will become mushy, and fish will toughen when left in marinade too long.

Marinate in a non-reactive container like ceramic, glass, or plastic, and place in the refrigerator. Metal dishes will corrode and give food a *tinny* flavor.

Before marinating meat, set a portion of the marinade aside to use as a basting sauce or to serve alongside the cooked meat. After soaking, discard any marinade used on raw meat.

MARINADES

Red Wine Marinade

This simple and flavorful marinade will transform beef or pork into a bistro-style classic.

1/4 cup red wine vinegar
1 tablespoon minced shallot
1 tablespoon honey
1 teaspoon Dijon mustard
1/3 cup olive oil

In 1-cup glass measure, whisk together all ingredients except olive oil. Whisking vigorously, add olive oil in slow, steady stream until well blended.

Makes about 2/3 cup

Tandoori Marinade

Add a little Indian spice to your barbecue with this tangy yogurt marinade. It's wonderful on chicken or pork.

1 carton (6 ounces) plain low-fat yogurt
1 tablespoon garam masala
1 tablespoon minced fresh ginger root
1 clove garlic, minced

In small bowl, stir together all ingredients.

Makes about 3/4 cup

TIP Garam masala is an Indian spice blend that adds spicy heat. Look for it in the spice aisle at Dierbergs.

Tuscan Marinade

Lots of lemon and garlic bring a little sun-drenched Mediterranean flavor to Tuscan Grilled Vegetables (page 73), beef, chicken, pork, salmon, or shrimp.

2 teaspoons grated lemon peel
1/4 cup fresh lemon juice
2 tablespoons olive oil
2 cloves garlic, minced
1 1/2 teaspoons Italian herb seasoning
1/2 teaspoon salt
1/4 teaspoon crushed red pepper flakes

In 1-cup glass measure, stir together all ingredients.

Makes about 1/2 cup

---

cuisine savvy

What is Tandoori?

Throughout India, cooks use outdoor brick ovens called *tandoors* to give foods a smoky flavor. Tandoori recipes almost always call for marinating meats in a blend of tangy yogurt and warm, fragrant spices.

It's easy to get a taste of tandoori right in your own backyard. Just fire up the grill! The most popular meat for this lively marinade is chicken, but it also makes pork deliciously tender and full of flavor.

BRINES

Basic Brine

This simple mixture is a great way to keep meat moist, tender, and juicy. Try it with beef brisket, chicken, pork, or shrimp. It makes Whiskey Pepper Chops (page 37) the best ever!

1 cup water
1/3 cup coarse salt
1/3 cup firmly packed brown sugar
2 cups ice water

In 2-cup glass measure, combine the 1 cup water, salt, and brown sugar. Microwave (high) for 2 minutes; stir until salt and sugar dissolve. Place 1-gallon freezer-weight reclosable plastic bag in large bowl or baking dish. Pour brine mixture into bag; add ice water. Add meat. Seal bag; refrigerate at least 8 hours or overnight. (Leave fish or seafood in brine for no longer than 30 minutes.) Remove meat from brine; discard brine. Grill meat according to recipe directions.

Makes about 3 cups

Beer Brine

Beer adds a tangy flavor that brings out the best in Sweet and Spicy Pork Steaks or Spareribs (recipes on page 30).

Basic Brine
   (see recipe above)
1 can (12 ounces) beer
1/2 cup dark corn syrup
1/4 cup Dijon mustard

Prepare Basic Brine according to directions. Add beer, corn syrup, and mustard. Add meat. Seal bag; refrigerate at least 8 hours or overnight. (Leave fish or seafood in brine for no longer than 30 minutes.) Remove meat from brine; discard brine. Grill meat according to recipe directions.

Makes about 5 cups

Java Brine

Add coffee and spices to Basic Brine for exotic flavor like you'll find in Java BBQ Chicken (page 44).

Basic Brine
   (see recipe above)
3/4 cup cold strong brewed coffee
1 tablespoon whole allspice
2 sticks cinnamon

Prepare Basic Brine according to directions. Add coffee, allspice, and cinnamon. Add meat. Seal bag; refrigerate at least 8 hours or overnight. Remove meat from brine; discard brine and whole spices. Grill meat according to recipe directions.

Makes about 4 cups

---

technique savvy
Brining 101

Brining is easy and a great way to increase the moisture content, add flavor, and keep meat, poultry, and seafood moist and juicy as they cook. Brining is always optional for a recipe, but well worth the effort. Follow brine recipes exactly to ensure balanced flavors and good texture.

Coarse or kosher salt is better for brines because it dissolves easily. If you use table salt, decrease the amount by about one-third.

Place a saucer or other clean object on top of the meat to keep it submerged. Refrigerate meats during brining. Avoid letting meat remain in the brine longer than the recipe directs. Once raw meat is removed from the brine, discard the brine and don't reuse it.

RUBS

Fresh Herb Rub

Plenty of garlic and fresh herbs make this fragrant rub perfect for beef, chicken, pork, or fish.

2 cloves garlic, minced
1 tablespoon snipped fresh rosemary
1 tablespoon snipped fresh thyme
1 tablespoon snipped fresh parsley
1 tablespoon coarse salt
1 tablespoon freshly ground black pepper

In small bowl, combine all ingredients. Rub onto meat before grilling.

Makes about 1/3 cup

Island Rub

Sprinkle on this lively mixture of warm Latin spices, pepper, and garlic. It's a great way to wake up beef, chicken, pork, or fish.

1 tablespoon chili powder
1 tablespoon ground cumin
1 teaspoon brown sugar
1 teaspoon ground coriander
1/2 teaspoon ground cinnamon
1/2 teaspoon garlic powder
1/2 teaspoon crushed red pepper flakes

In small bowl, combine all ingredients. Rub onto meat before grilling.

Makes about 1/4 cup

Southwest Rub

This unlikely blend of seasonings is pure magic! Rub it onto beef, chicken, pork, or fish for a savory touch that's spiced just right.

1/4 cup brown sugar
1 tablespoon chili powder
1 tablespoon instant espresso powder
1 teaspoon paprika
1 teaspoon dried rosemary
1 teaspoon coarse salt
1 teaspoon freshly ground black pepper

In small bowl, combine all ingredients. Rub onto meat before grilling.

Makes about 1/2 cup

TIP For added flavor, use ancho chile powder and Hungarian sweet paprika.

---

technique savvy

Rubs 101

Whether you follow a recipe or create your own, these savory mixtures of spices and seasonings can work magic on just about anything you care to put on the grill. Rubbed onto the surface of meats and vegetables, rubs add loads of flavor.

Dry rubs are usually combinations of dried herbs, spices, and seasonings, and often contain sugar to help form a nice crust. Use fresh chopped herbs instead of dried and add a little oil or other liquid to make a paste or a wet rub.

Apply rubs to meat just before grilling or place the seasoned meat in the refrigerator for an hour or so to let flavors develop. Salt and sugar can draw moisture out of food, so apply the rub according to recipe directions.

DIERBERGS SCHOOL OF COOKING

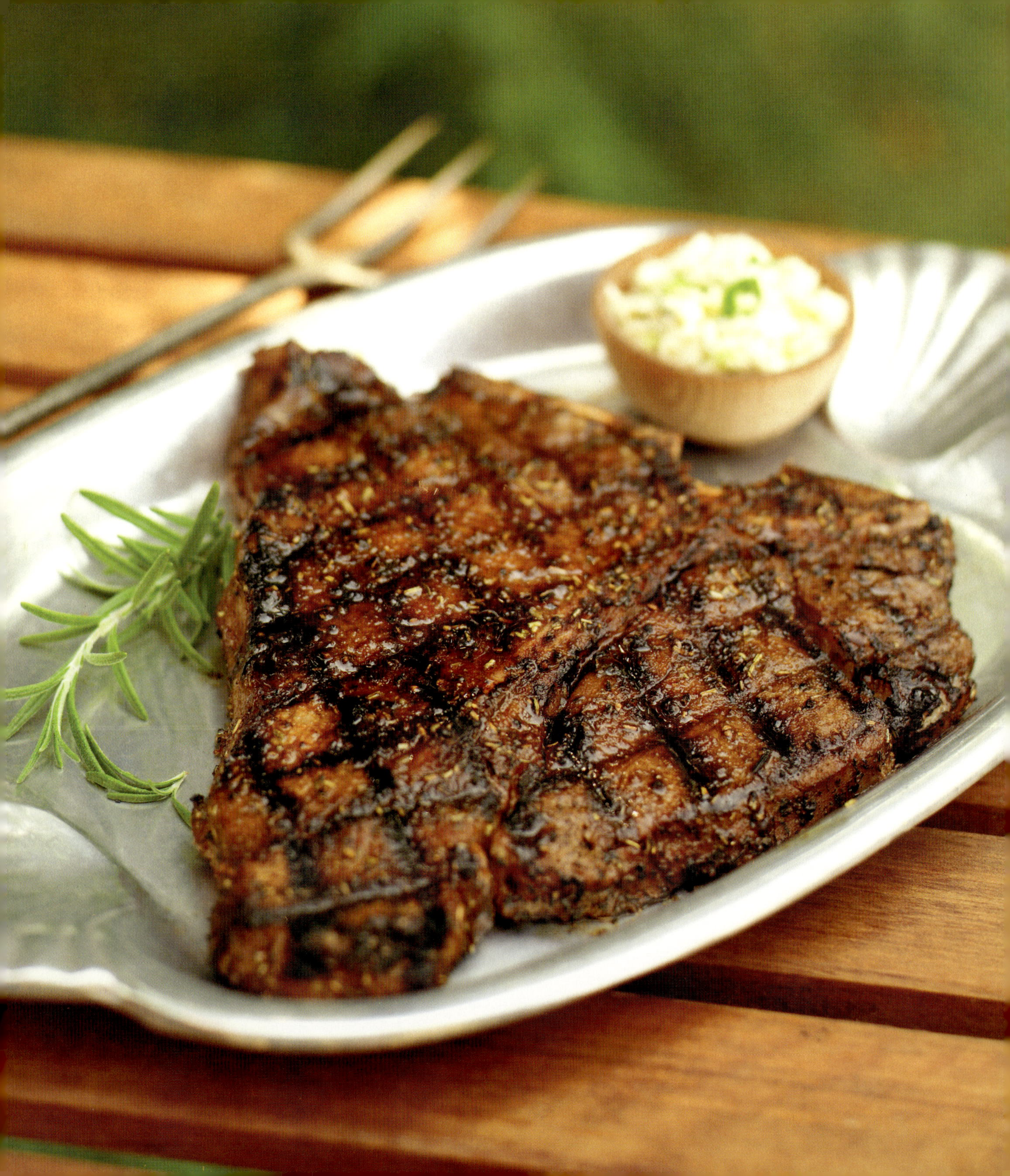

beef & pork

Chicago-Style Steaks with Blue Cheese Butter	20
Santa Fe Tostadas with Chipotle Sour Cream	21
Steak Fajitas with Pico de Gallo	23
Balsamic Grilled Sirloin	24
Petite Tenders with Greek Herbed Tomato Salad	24
Pickapeppa Beef Kabobs	26
Mesquite Smoked Brisket	28
Beef and Portabella Burgers	29
Sweet and Spicy Spareribs	30
Maple Mustard Pork Roast	31
Rubbed Pork Tenderloin with Mango Bourbon Sauce	32
Asian Barbecued Pork Wraps	34
Raspberry Balsamic Pork on Greens	35
Whiskey Pepper Chops with Molasses Butter	37
Margarita Glazed Pork Chops	38
Italian Sausage and Pasta Grill	39

◀ *Chicago-Style Steaks with Blue Cheese Butter*
Recipe on page 20

Chicago-Style Steaks with Blue Cheese Butter

Dierbergs School of Cooking Manager Nancy Lorenz is our "entrée specialist." Dust a porterhouse or T-bone with her savory rub and top it with luscious blue cheese butter to bring classic steak house flavors to your table.

1 tablespoon brown sugar
1/2 teaspoon garlic powder
1/2 teaspoon paprika
1/2 teaspoon dried rosemary, crushed
1/2 teaspoon dried oregano
1/4 teaspoon coarse salt
1/4 teaspoon freshly ground black pepper
2 bone-in beef porterhouse or T-bone steaks, 1 inch thick (about 1 1/2 pounds each)
Blue Cheese Butter

In small bowl, combine brown sugar and seasonings. Rub evenly onto both sides of steaks. Place steaks on oiled grid over medium-high heat; cover and grill until internal temperature is 145°F. for medium, about 6 to 7 minutes per side. Cover and let stand 10 minutes before cutting into serving-size pieces. Serve with Blue Cheese Butter.

Makes 4 servings

TIP You can substitute any tender steak, like fillet, rib-eye, sirloin, or strip.

Blue Cheese Butter

2 tablespoons butter, softened
2 tablespoons crumbled blue cheese
2 tablespoons thinly sliced green onion

In small bowl, stir together all ingredients. Chill several hours or overnight to develop flavors.

Makes about 1/4 cup

Per 1 tablespoon Calories 67; Fat 7 g; Cholesterol 19 mg; Sodium 49 mg; Carbohydrate <1 g; Fiber <1 g

---

ingredient savvy
Steaks

Steaks are among the most popular fresh beef cuts. The most tender steaks include porterhouse, T-bone, strip, rib-eye, and filet mignon. Whether you season them or throw them on the grill as-is, they cook up juicy and delicious.

Some of the less expensive steaks are less tender, but they are very flavorful. Less tender steaks include London broil, flank, skirt, and chuck. A few hours (from 2 to 24 hours) in the refrigerator in a flavorful marinade is time well spent. Slice them thinly across the grain for the best texture.

Per serving with 1 tablespoon Blue Cheese Butter

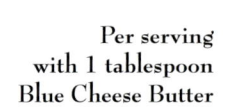

Calories 651
Fat 44 g
Cholesterol 166 mg
Sodium 291 mg
Carbohydrate 4 g
Fiber <1 g

GREG'S GRILLING TIP

When you throw steaks on the grill, here's how to make crosshatch grill marks. Put the steaks diagonally on a preheated oiled grid, and let them cook for about 3 minutes. Then rotate them 90 degrees and cook another 3 minutes on the same side. Turn them over, and grill until they are done.

Santa Fe Tostadas with Chipotle Sour Cream

Spread a crispy, grilled tortilla with a smoky chile sour cream sauce. Then top it with zesty steak strips and all the trimmings for a fast fiesta any night of the week.

1 beef sirloin, flank, or London broil steak (about 1 1/2 pounds) 1/4 cup fresh lime juice 2 cloves garlic, minced 2 tablespoons honey 1 tablespoon chipotle purée 1 teaspoon ground cumin 1/2 teaspoon salt 1/4 cup olive oil 8 flour tortillas (8-inch diameter) Olive oil Chipotle Sour Cream Shredded iceberg lettuce 1 avocado, pitted, peeled, and thinly sliced 1/3 cup finely chopped red onion Fresh cilantro	Place steak in large freezer-weight reclosable plastic bag. In 1-cup glass measure, whisk together lime juice, garlic, honey, chipotle purée, cumin, and salt. Whisking vigorously, add the 1/4 cup olive oil in slow, steady stream until well blended. Pour over steak; seal bag and turn to coat meat. Place bag on plate and marinate in refrigerator for several hours or overnight. Remove steak from bag; discard marinade. Place steak on grid over medium-high heat; cover and grill until internal temperature is 145°F. for medium, about 5 to 7 minutes per side. Cover and let stand 10 minutes before thinly slicing across the grain. Brush both sides of each tortilla with olive oil. Place on grid over medium-high heat; grill until golden brown and crisp, about 1 to 2 minutes per side. If tortillas bubble up, pierce surface to flatten. Spread grilled tortilla with dollop of Chipotle Sour Cream, leaving 1-inch border. Top with lettuce, beef slices, avocado, onion, and cilantro. Serve with additional Chipotle Sour Cream. Makes 8 servings

Chipotle Sour Cream

1 container (8 ounces) dairy sour cream 2 teaspoons fresh lime juice 2 teaspoons chipotle purée 1 teaspoon honey 1/4 teaspoon ground cumin 1/4 teaspoon salt	In small bowl, stir together all ingredients. Chill for several hours or up to 2 days to develop flavors. Makes about 1 cup Per 2 tablespoons Calories 65; Fat 6 g; Cholesterol 13 mg; Sodium 98 mg; Carbohydrate 2 g; Fiber 0 g

---

ingredient savvy

Chipotles in Adobo Sauce

Purchase chipotles in adobo sauce in the Mexican food section. Purée the chiles with the sauce and place in a freezer-weight plastic bag. Lay flat and freeze so you can break off a piece as needed to add a touch of smoky heat to all sorts of dishes.

Per serving with 2 tablespoons Chipotle Sour Cream

Calories 397
Fat 17 g
Cholesterol 89 mg
Sodium 303 mg
Carbohydrate 29 g
Fiber 3 g

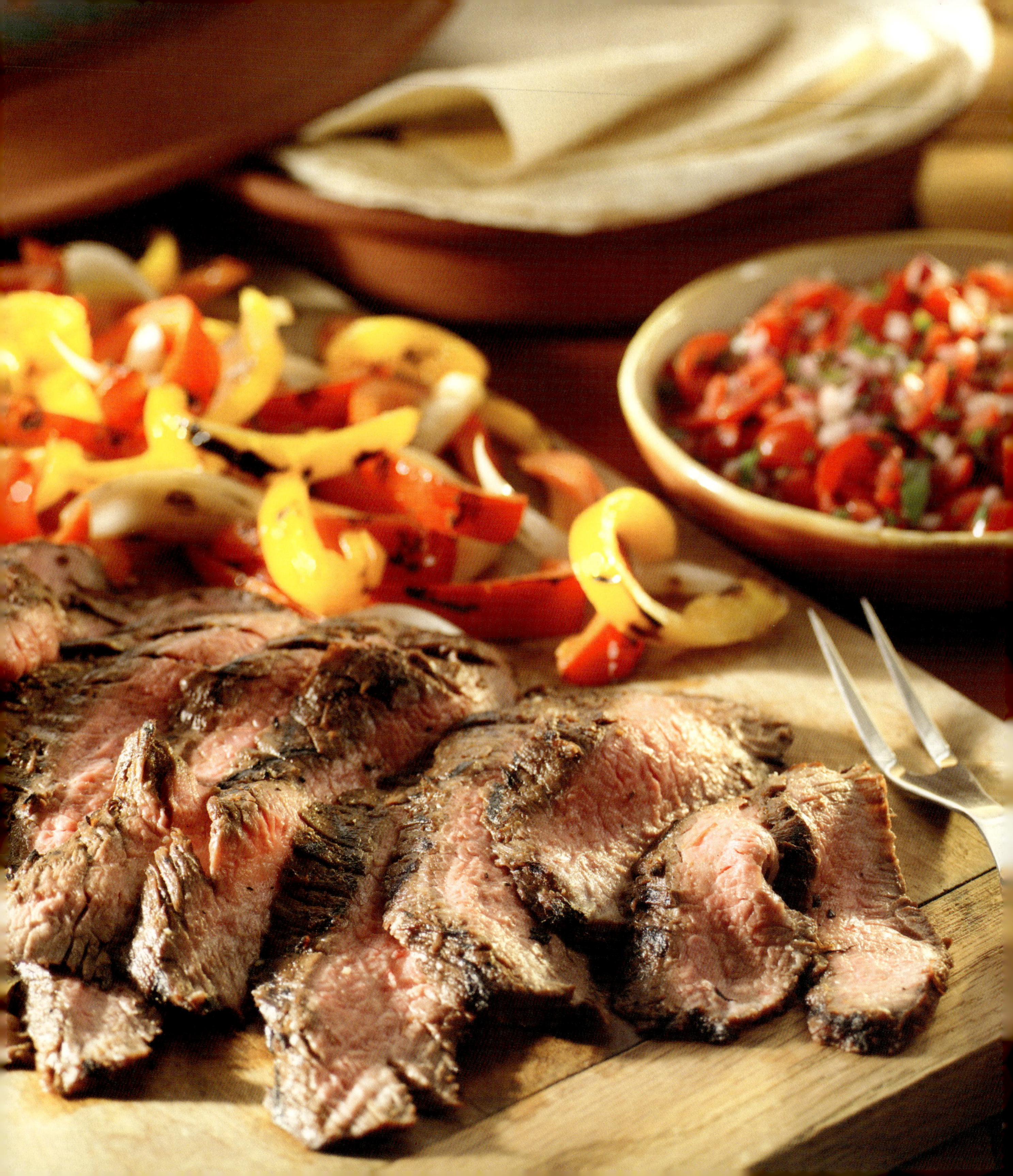

Steak Fajitas with Pico de Gallo

According to Cathy Chipley, co-host of Dierbergs Presents Everybody Cooks® TV show, the terrific marinade is what makes these fajitas really special. She serves them with a chunky Pico de Gallo (PEE-coh day GI-yoh) for an authentic touch.

1 beef sirloin, flank, or London broil steak (about 1½ to 2 pounds)
¼ cup fresh lime juice
2 tablespoons olive oil
2 tablespoons honey
2 teaspoons chipotle purée (see *Chipotles in Adobo Sauce* on page 21)
2 teaspoons ground cumin
4 cloves garlic, minced
Salt and pepper to taste
2 large bell peppers, quartered and seeded
1 large onion, cut into wedges
Olive oil
12 flour tortillas (8-inch diameter), warmed
Pico de Gallo

Place steak in large freezer-weight reclosable plastic bag. In 2-cup glass measure, whisk together lime juice, olive oil, honey, chipotle purée, cumin, and garlic. Pour over steak; seal bag and turn to coat meat. Place bag on plate and marinate in refrigerator for several hours or overnight. Remove steak from bag; discard marinade.

Season steak with salt and pepper. Place steak on grid over medium-high heat; cover and grill until internal temperature is 145°F. for medium, about 5 to 7 minutes per side. Cover and let stand 10 minutes before thinly slicing across the grain.

Brush vegetables with olive oil. Place on grid over medium-high heat; grill turning frequently and brushing with oil as needed until crisp-tender and lightly charred, about 8 to 10 minutes. Cut vegetables into strips. Divide vegetables and beef among tortillas; top with Pico de Gallo.

Makes 6-8 servings

TIP Substitute 1½ to 2 pounds boneless, skinless chicken breast halves that have been pounded to even thickness for the beef steak.

Pico de Gallo

1½ cups chopped tomato
½ cup minced red onion
1 jalapeño, halved, seeded, deveined, and minced
¼ cup snipped fresh cilantro
1 tablespoon fresh lime juice
Salt and pepper to taste

In medium bowl, stir together tomato, onion, jalapeño, cilantro, and lime juice. Season with salt and pepper. Let stand for 15 minutes to develop flavors.

Makes about 2 cups

Per 2 tablespoons Calories 6; Fat 0 g; Cholesterol 0 mg; Sodium 2 mg; Carbohydrate 1 g; Fiber <1 g

---

technique savvy

Set Up a Fajita Bar

Not so very long ago, no one outside of Texas had ever heard of fajitas. Sizzling strips of grilled steak, onions, and peppers wrapped up in warm flour tortillas are now a favorite from coast to coast.

For a fun and easy dinner, set up a fajita bar. Grill marinated steak and chicken breasts along with bell peppers and onions. While everything cooks, warm a stack of flour tortillas. Just wrap them in foil, and set them off to the side of the grill. Be sure to turn the foil packet occasionally.

Then cut the meat and vegetables into strips and arrange on platters. Set out bowls of guacamole, salsa, cheese, sour cream, Pico de Gallo – any toppings you like – and let everyone build the fajita of their dreams.

Per serving

Calories 377
Fat 8 g
Cholesterol 76 mg
Sodium 258 mg
Carbohydrate 43 g
Fiber 3 g

Balsamic Grilled Sirloin

Capture the great flavors of the corner bistro with this savory steak. A tangy balsamic marinade and a sprinkle of fragrant French herbs make a great steak even better.

Per serving

Calories 230
Fat 9 g
Cholesterol 101 mg
Sodium 75 mg
Carbohydrate <1 g
Fiber 0 g

1 beef sirloin steak (about 1½ pounds)
Balsamic Marinade (recipe on page 14)
1 teaspoon herbes de Provence
Salt and pepper to taste

Place steak in large freezer-weight reclosable plastic bag. Pour Marinade over steak; seal bag and turn to coat meat. Place bag on plate and marinate in refrigerator for several hours or overnight. Remove steak from bag; discard marinade.

Season steak with herbes de Provence, salt, and pepper. Place steak on grid over medium-high heat; cover and grill until internal temperature is 145°F. for medium, about 5 to 7 minutes per side. Cover and let stand 10 minutes before cutting into serving-size pieces.

Makes 6 servings

Petite Tenders with Greek Herbed Tomato Salad

As tender as beef tenderloin but at a much more popular price, beef petite shoulder tender is a deliciously affordable splurge. Keep the seasonings simple and team it with a terrific tomato salad for an easy and elegant meal.

Per serving

Calories 318
Fat 22 g
Cholesterol 73 mg
Sodium 364 mg
Carbohydrate 6 g
Fiber <1 g

1½ pounds beef petite shoulder tender
1 tablespoon olive oil
Coarse salt and freshly ground black pepper to taste
Greek Herbed Tomato Salad (recipe on page 67)

Trim and discard fat and silver skin from beef. Brush meat with olive oil; season with salt and pepper. Place beef on grid over medium-high heat; cover and grill turning occasionally until internal temperature is 145°F. for medium, about 20 to 25 minutes. Cover and let stand 10 minutes before slicing. Serve with Greek Herbed Tomato Salad spooned over top.

Makes 4-6 servings

TIP Silver skin is a thin membrane that covers petite tenders. Remove and discard it before cooking to make the meat more tender and prevent it from curling. Use a sharp knife to loosen the silver skin and gently scrape it away.

Petite Tenders with Greek Herbed Tomato Salad ▶

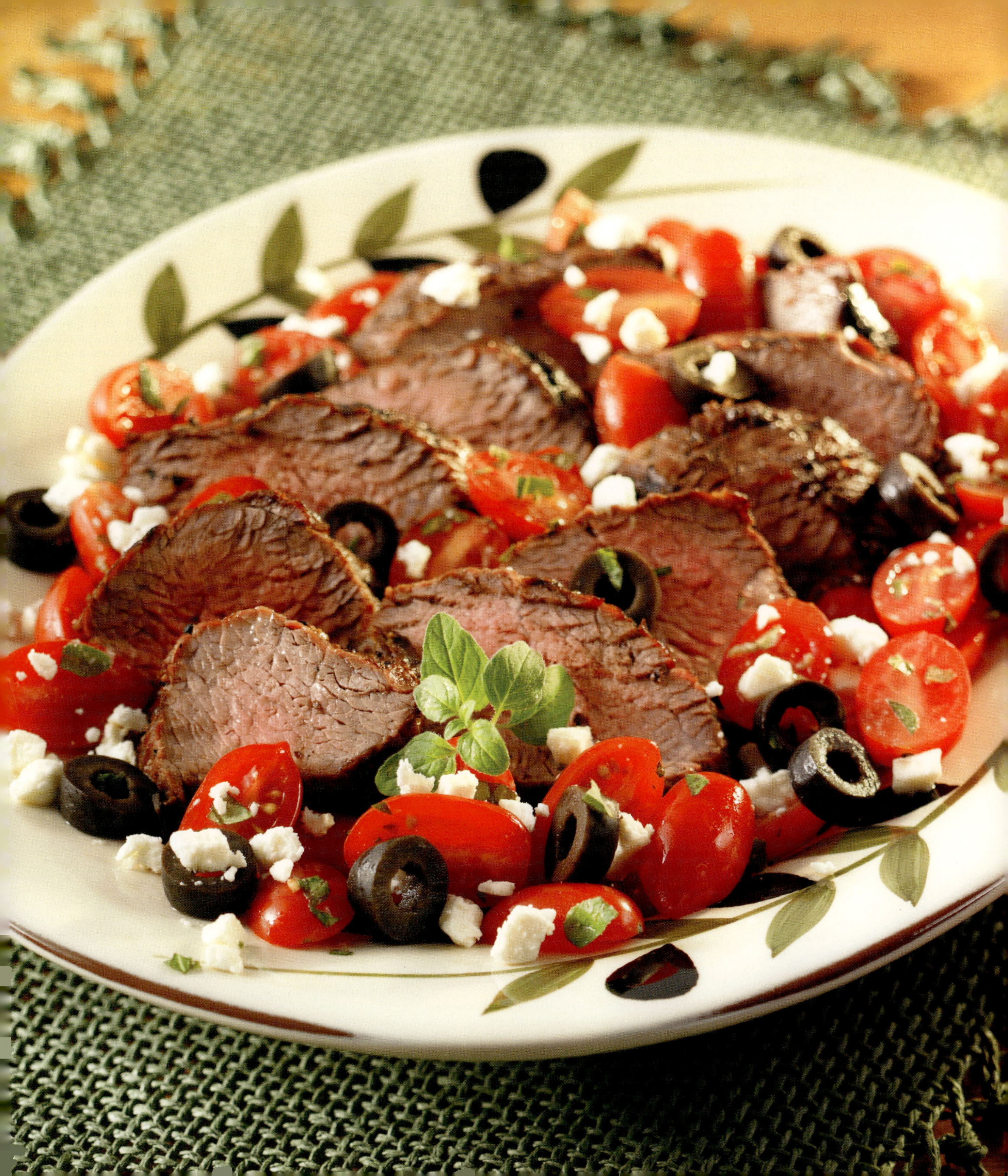

Pickapeppa Beef Kabobs

Dinner on a stick is just plain fun! Skewer up chunks of tender beef and colorful vegetables, then brush on a savory glaze for a quick and delicious dinner. Try all of the tasty variations, too!

technique savvy
Kabob Klues

Soak bamboo skewers in water for at least 30 minutes before using to prevent burning.

Choose bamboo skewers for smaller, softer foods, and metal skewers for firm foods like potatoes.

Skewer foods with similar cooking times together, cutting them into similar-size pieces for even cooking.

Leave a little space between foods as you place them on skewers.

Choose flat or square metal skewers to prevent food from twirling; or thread food onto 2 parallel skewers (see *Step-by-Step Instructions* on page 53).

- 1½ pounds beef petite shoulder tender or sirloin steak
- 2 red bell peppers, seeded and cut into 1-inch pieces
- 1 red onion, cut into wedges
- 1 medium zucchini, cut into chunks
- Wooden skewers, soaked in water for 30 minutes
- Olive oil
- Pickapeppa Glaze (recipe on page 13)

Cut beef into 1-inch cubes. Alternately thread beef and vegetables onto skewers; lightly brush with oil. Place skewers on grid over medium-high heat; cover and grill, turning and basting with Glaze until meat is browned and vegetables are crisp-tender, about 10 minutes.

Makes 6 servings

VARIATIONS

Chili Cherry Pork Kabobs Substitute 1½ pounds boneless pork loin, cut into 1-inch cubes, for the beef; and Chili Cherry Sauce (recipe on page 12) for the Pickapeppa Glaze.

Per serving Calories 321; Fat 14 g; Cholesterol 59 mg; Sodium 290 mg; Carbohydrate 28 g; Fiber 2 g

Caribbean Chicken Kabobs Substitute 1½ pounds boneless, skinless chicken breast halves, cut into 1-inch cubes, for the beef; and Caribbean Glaze (recipe on page 13) for the Pickapeppa Glaze.

Per serving Calories 232; Fat 1 g; Cholesterol 43 mg; Sodium 297 mg; Carbohydrate 33 g; Fiber 1 g

Per serving

Calories 188
Fat 6 g
Cholesterol 66 mg
Sodium 182 mg
Carbohydrate 11 g
Fiber 1 g

GREG'S GRILLING TIP *Sweet basting sauces are a favorite, but they burn like crazy, so don't brush them on food until the last 10 minutes or so of cooking time.*

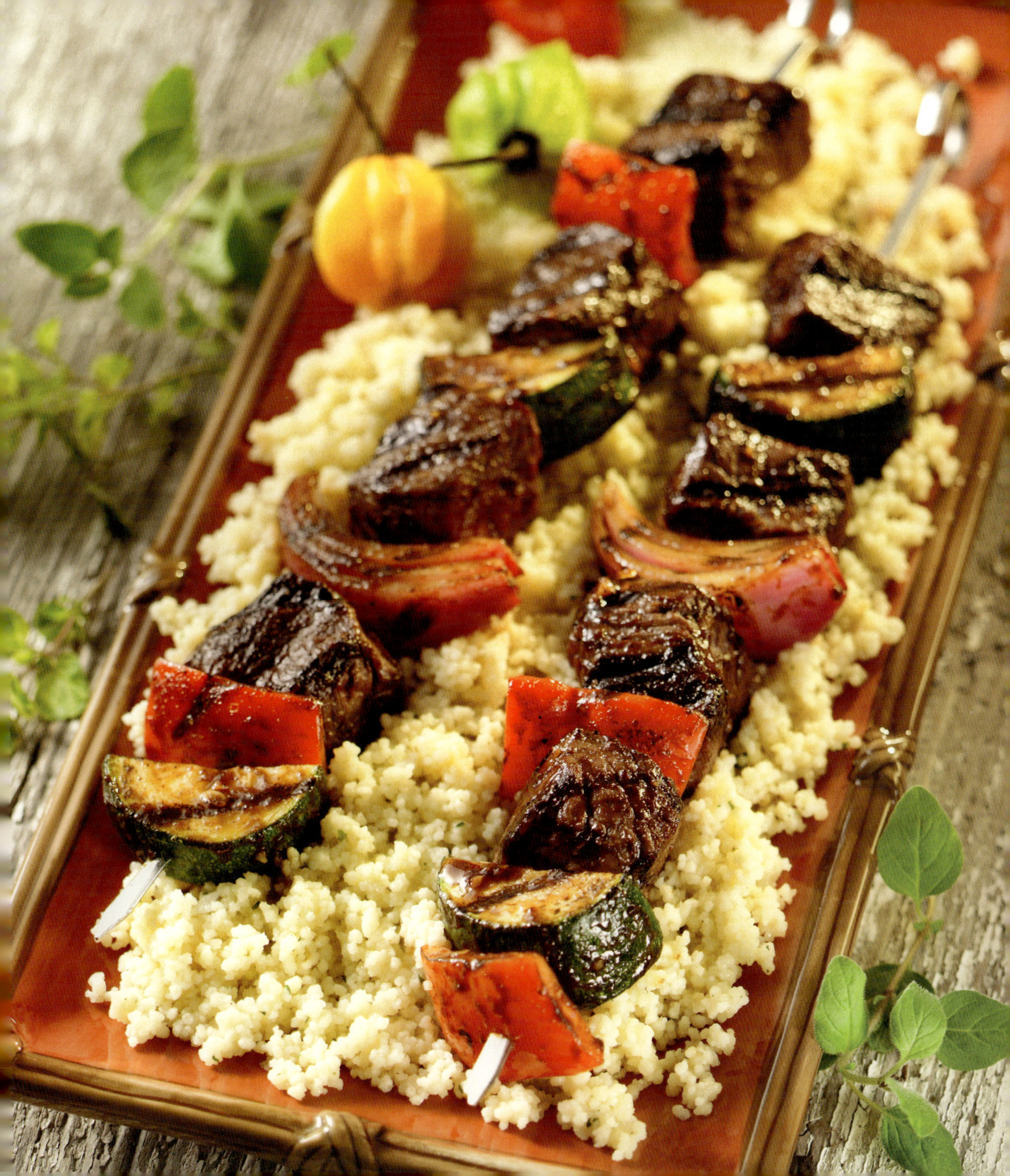

technique savvy

Where There's Smoke…

…there's flavor. The aroma of meat slowly smoking on the grill will drive the neighbors wild.

Start by building an indirect fire (see *Indirect-Heat Grilling* on page 7). Next, soak hardwood chips in water for at least 30 minutes to let the aroma release more slowly. For charcoal fires, sprinkle soaked chips directly onto the coals. For gas grills, place soaked chips in a disposable foil pan on top of the burner.

Use a small amount of wood chips to see how you like the flavor. The more chips you use, the stronger the flavor will be.

Per serving

Calories 154
Fat 4 g
Cholesterol 47 mg
Sodium 142 mg
Carbohydrate 1 g
Fiber 0 g

Mesquite Smoked Brisket

The spicy whiskey marinade makes this tender brisket a real crowd pleaser. Serve it on buns for a terrific sandwich.

1 flat-cut beef brisket (about 4 to 5 pounds)
½ cup whiskey or red wine vinegar
½ cup Dijon mustard
2 tablespoons seasoned pepper medley
6 cups mesquite chips, soaked in water for 30 minutes

Trim visible fat from brisket. Place brisket in large freezer-weight reclosable plastic bag. In 2-cup glass measure, combine whiskey, mustard, and pepper. Pour over brisket; seal bag and turn to coat meat. Place bag on plate and marinate in refrigerator for 24 hours. Remove brisket from bag; discard marinade.

Prepare grill for medium-high indirect heat (see *Indirect-Heat Grilling* on page 7). Add ⅓ of the mesquite chips (see sidebar). Place brisket on oiled grid; cover and smoke for 1 hour, adding additional mesquite chips every 20 minutes.

Place brisket on large sheet of heavy-duty foil. Bring sides of foil to center in series of locked folds; fold up ends to seal completely. Place packet on grid over medium indirect heat; cover and grill until meat is very tender, about 1½ to 2 hours. (Add coals as needed to maintain medium heat.) Carefully open foil packet to reserve juice; place brisket on cutting board. Cover and let stand 10 minutes before thinly slicing across the grain. Serve with reserved juice.

Makes 10-12 servings

GREG'S GRILLING TIP

Wood chips add great flavor to food, but use them sparingly. Too much smoke can overpower food and make it taste bitter. Be sure to use a meat thermometer to determine doneness (see Thermometers *on page 9). Smoked meats often look pink even though they're done.*

Beef and Portabella Burgers

Calling all mushroom lovers! We put savory sautéed portabella mushrooms in these beefy burgers for a rich, earthy flavor in every bite.

2 portabella mushrooms
1 teaspoon olive oil
1 cup chopped onion
1/2 teaspoon dried thyme
1/4 cup Worcestershire sauce
1 pound lean ground beef
1 egg, slightly beaten, OR
 1/4 cup egg substitute
1/2 teaspoon salt
1/4 teaspoon ground black pepper
1 loaf (8 ounces) Dierbergs bakery baguette
Olive oil no-stick cooking spray

Remove and discard stems and gills from mushrooms (see *Step-by-Step Instructions* on page 74); coarsely chop caps. In large skillet, heat olive oil over medium-high heat. Add mushrooms, onion, and thyme; cover and cook for 4 minutes. Add Worcestershire sauce; cook for 2 minutes. Cool completely.

In large bowl, combine ground beef, egg, salt, pepper, and mushroom mixture. Shape beef mixture into 6 patties. Place on grid over medium-high heat; cover and grill until internal temperature is 165°F., about 5 to 6 minutes per side.

Cut bread diagonally into twelve 1/2-inch-thick slices. (Save remaining bread for other uses.) Lightly coat cut-sides of bread with cooking spray. Place on oiled grid over medium-high heat; grill until lightly toasted and grill marks appear, about 1 to 2 minutes per side. Serve burgers on toasted baguette slices.

Makes 6 servings

GREG'S GRILLING TIP *Never turn your back when you're grilling sliced bread. It will turn from perfect toast to a charred mess in just a few seconds, and burnt toast doesn't smell any better outside than it does in your kitchen!*

technique savvy

Burger Basics

Everybody loves a big, juicy burger hot off the grill. Give them a little TLC, and you'll have perfect burgers every time.

Season the meat with salt, pepper, and any other seasonings you like. Dampen hands with water, and shape patties gently without compacting the meat. Over-handling will make burgers dry and cause them to shrink.

Burgers start out flat but often puff up into balls as they cook. To make sure that patties stay flat, don't smash them with a spatula as they cook. Instead, press the center of each patty down to make an imprint *before* you put burgers on the grill.

For food safety, cook burgers over direct heat until well done in the center.

Per serving

Calories 229
Fat 7 g
Cholesterol 82 mg
Sodium 503 mg
Carbohydrate 16 g
Fiber 1 g

Sweet and Spicy Spareribs

Brining makes the most succulent ribs you'll ever eat. Try it on pork steaks, too.

technique savvy

Step-by-Step Instructions

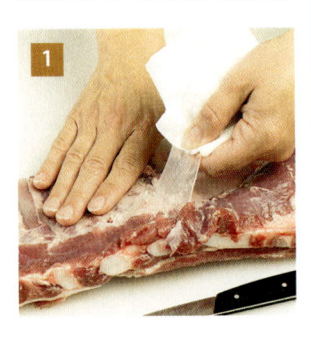

2 slabs pork spareribs
   (about 2 pounds each)
Beer Brine
   (recipe on page 16)
½ cup Best-Ever Barbecue
   Sauce (recipe on page 12)

1 Slide sharp knife under tough membrane covering back of ribs. Loosen membrane at one end of slab. Use paper towel to grasp loosened membrane firmly and pull off. Place ribs in 2-gallon freezer-weight reclosable plastic bag; place bag in large bowl or baking dish. Pour brine over ribs. Seal bag; refrigerate at least 8 hours or overnight. Remove ribs from brine and pat dry; discard brine.

Place ribs bone-sides together on large sheet of heavy-duty foil. Bring sides of foil to center in series of locked folds, allowing space for steam; fold up ends to seal completely. Place packet on grid over medium-high indirect heat (see *Indirect-Heat Grilling* on page 7); cover and grill turning every 10 to 15 minutes until very tender, about 1½ hours. (Add coals as needed to maintain medium-high heat.) Remove ribs from foil. Place ribs directly on grid over medium heat. Grill turning frequently and basting with Sauce until glazed, about 10 minutes.

Makes 4-6 servings

VARIATION

Sweet and Spicy Pork Steaks Substitute 4 to 6 center-cut pork steaks for the ribs. Brine as directed. Place on grid over medium heat; grill turning frequently and basting with Sauce during last 15 minutes of cooking until tender, about 30 to 35 minutes.

Per serving Calories 359; Fat 21 g; Cholesterol 105 mg; Sodium 887 mg; Carbohydrate 11 g; Fiber <1 g

Per serving

Calories 548
Fat 39 g
Cholesterol 141 mg
Sodium 929 mg
Carbohydrate 11 g
Fiber <1 g

Maple Mustard Pork Roast

Two simple ingredients make one terrific glaze for pork. Serve the Sassy Cider Sauce alongside.

1 boneless center-cut pork loin roast (about 2 pounds)
¼ cup pure maple syrup
2 tablespoons coarse Dijon mustard

Trim and discard fat from roast. In 1-cup glass measure, stir together maple syrup and mustard. Place roast on oiled grid over medium indirect heat (see *Indirect-Heat Grilling* on page 7); cover and grill for 15 minutes. Brush maple syrup mixture over roast. Cover and grill turning occasionally until internal temperature is 150°F., about 45 to 60 minutes. Cover and let stand 10 minutes before slicing. Serve with Sassy Cider Sauce.

Makes 6 servings

Sassy Cider Sauce

1 cup apple cider or juice
2 tablespoons pure maple syrup
1 tablespoon coarse Dijon mustard
1 tablespoon cornstarch, dissolved in 1 tablespoon water

In small saucepan, combine apple cider, maple syrup, and mustard over medium-high heat; bring to a boil. Reduce heat and whisk in cornstarch mixture; cook until thickened, about 2 minutes.

Makes about 1 cup

Per 2 tablespoons Calories 33; Fat 0 g; Cholesterol 0 mg; Sodium 47 mg; Carbohydrate 8 g; Fiber 0 g

GREG'S GRILLING TIP
Stock up on disposable foil pans. They're great for catching drips when you cook food over indirect heat, and there's nothing to clean up.

---

technique savvy

Different Smokes for Different Folks

Different species of wood lend different flavors to food. The familiar flavor of hickory is strong and smoky, ideal for beef, pork, and chicken. Pecan is rich, but milder than hickory, and pairs well with pork, chicken, and fish. Beef and mesquite are a classic combo. Mesquite burns hot, so use it sparingly.

Cedar is a traditional choice for smoking salmon and other fish, chicken, and pork because of its delicate flavor. No surprise, cherry and apple have a sweet, fruity flavor that's perfect with pork and poultry.

To add wood smoke to your grill, see *Where There's Smoke* on page 28.

Per serving with 2 tablespoons Sassy Cider Sauce

Calories 247
Fat 7 g
Cholesterol 64 mg
Sodium 215 mg
Carbohydrate 18 g
Fiber 0 g

Rubbed Pork Tenderloin with Mango Bourbon Sauce

Dierbergs School of Cooking instructor, Chef Jack West MacMurray III of Sage Urban-American Grill, knows how to create maximum impact with everyday ingredients. A zesty rub and sassy sauce take pork tenderloin to a new level.

technique savvy

Step-by-Step Instructions

1

2

Per serving

Calories 233
Fat 5 g
Cholesterol 84 mg
Sodium 676 mg
Carbohydrate 14 g
Fiber 1 g

---

2 pork tenderloins (about 1 1/4 pounds each)
1 tablespoon brown sugar
2 teaspoons coarse salt
2 teaspoons ground cumin
1 teaspoon garlic powder
1 teaspoon freshly ground black pepper
1/2 teaspoon chipotle chile powder
Mango Bourbon Sauce

Mango Bourbon Sauce

1 mango
1 tablespoon olive oil
1/2 cup diced onion
1/2 cup chopped red bell pepper
2 tablespoons minced garlic
1/2 cup ketchup
1/4 cup firmly packed brown sugar
1/4 cup apple cider vinegar
2 tablespoons hoisin sauce
1 tablespoon fresh lime juice
1 teaspoon chipotle chile powder
1/3 cup bourbon

Trim and discard fat and silver skin from tenderloins. Cut pork into 1-inch-thick medallions; flatten slightly with heel of hand. In small bowl, combine remaining ingredients except Sauce. Season both sides of medallions with rub mixture.

Remove 1/2 cup Mango Bourbon Sauce to baste pork; reserve remaining Sauce to serve with pork. Place medallions on oiled grid over medium-high heat; cover and grill basting occasionally with Sauce until no longer pink, about 4 minutes per side. Serve with reserved Mango Bourbon Sauce spooned over top.

Makes 8 servings

1 Hold mango stem-end up on cutting board. Make vertical slice along one of the long sides, about 3/8 inch from stem, following curve of seed. Make second slice on other side, about 3/8 inch from stem. (The long seed will be in center slice.) Place double layer of clean kitchen towel in your hand. Hold one of the slices in your hand. Using tip of sharp knife, score mango into 3/4-inch cubes, being careful not to cut through peel. Push up on center to turn mango inside-out. **2** Run knife just above mango skin to slice away cubes. Repeat procedure with other mango half. Cut remaining mango away from seed and peel; cut into cubes.

In large saucepan, heat olive oil over medium-high heat. Add onion, bell pepper, and garlic; cook until onion wilts. Add mango and remaining ingredients except bourbon. Reduce heat and simmer for 30 minutes. Stir in bourbon. Cool to room temperature. In work bowl of food processor fitted with steel knife blade, process sauce mixture until smooth.

Makes 2 1/2 cups

Per 2 tablespoons Calories 46; Fat 1 g; Cholesterol 0 mg; Sodium 96 mg; Carbohydrate 8 g; Fiber <1 g

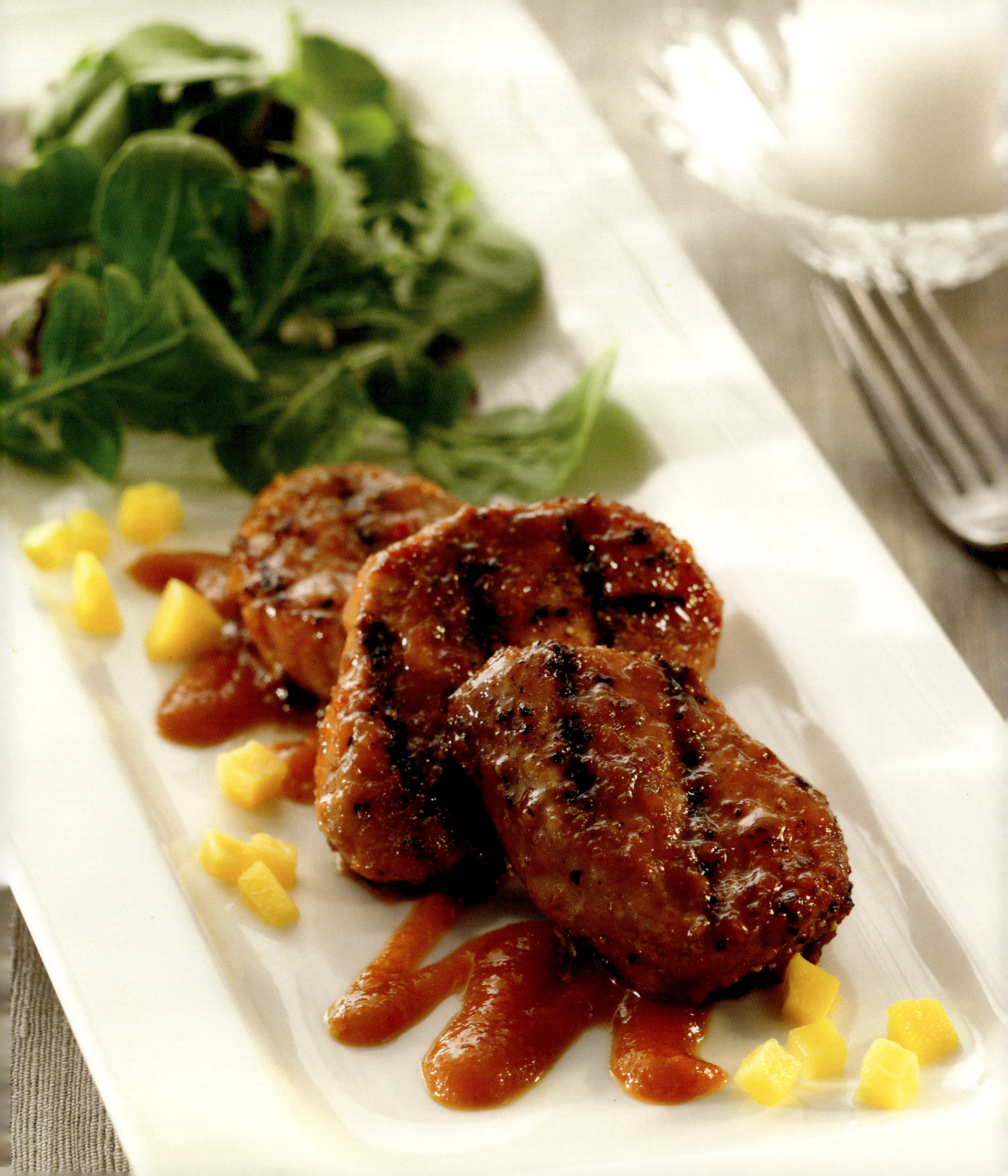

Asian Barbecued Pork Wraps

Here's an Asian take on the classic Southern barbecue sandwich combo of tender pork and crunchy slaw. Some things are good in any language!

1 pork tenderloin (about 1¼ pounds)
¼ cup hoisin sauce
2 tablespoons brown sugar
2 tablespoons soy sauce
2 tablespoons dark sesame oil
1 tablespoon dry sherry
2 cloves garlic, minced
¼ teaspoon crushed red pepper flakes
6 flour tortillas (8-inch diameter), warmed
Asian Slaw (recipe on page 72)

Trim and discard fat and silver skin from tenderloin. Cut pork into 1-inch-thick medallions; flatten slightly with heel of hand. Place medallions in large freezer-weight reclosable plastic bag. In 1-cup glass measure, stir together hoisin sauce, brown sugar, soy sauce, sesame oil, sherry, garlic, and pepper flakes. Pour over medallions; seal bag and turn to coat meat. Place bag on plate and marinate in refrigerator for several hours or overnight. Remove medallions from bag; discard marinade.

Place medallions on oiled grid over medium-high heat; cover and grill until no longer pink, about 4 minutes per side. Cut medallions into strips; place on tortillas. Top each with ¼ cup of the Asian Slaw. Roll up tortillas; secure each end with wooden pick. Cut tortillas in half diagonally. Serve with remaining Asian Slaw.

Makes 6 servings

GREG'S GRILLING TIP
Nobody wants barbecue that's dry and chewy, so ditch the fork and turn food with a pair of tongs. Forks leave holes that let juices escape, which makes food dry.

---

technique savvy
Weather or Not

Grilling isn't just for warm, sunny days – it's for everyday! Aside from a thunderstorm, don't let less-than-beautiful weather keep you from firing up the grill.

On cold days, brush off any snow and allow more time to preheat the grill. You'll need a few extra minutes of cooking time, too.

Windy days affect grilling as well. Position gas grill so the wind doesn't blow into burners and snuff out flames. If flames go out, turn off the burners and wait 5 minutes before re-lighting.

If you use charcoal, keep the vents open. You may need to add briquettes to maintain fire temperature. And in any kind of weather, keep the lid closed as much as possible to keep heat in.

Per serving

Calories 261
Fat 6 g
Cholesterol 58 mg
Sodium 339 mg
Carbohydrate 28 g
Fiber 1 g

Raspberry Balsamic Pork on Greens

A simple sweet and tangy marinade doubles as a salad dressing in this fast and fabulous entrée. It's easy enough for a weeknight meal and special enough for guests.

1 pork tenderloin (about 1¼ pounds)
¼ cup seedless raspberry jam
¼ cup balsamic vinegar
2 tablespoons olive oil
1 clove garlic, minced
½ teaspoon dried thyme
¼ teaspoon ground black pepper
8 cups mixed salad greens
¼ cup thinly sliced sweet onion (Maui, Vidalia, red)
Fresh raspberries

Trim and discard fat and silver skin from tenderloin. Place pork in large freezer-weight reclosable plastic bag. In 1-cup glass measure, stir together jam, vinegar, oil, garlic, thyme, and pepper. Pour half of the mixture over pork; reserve remaining mixture for dressing. Seal bag; turn to coat meat. Place bag on plate and marinate in refrigerator for 2 to 4 hours. Remove pork from bag; discard marinade.

Place tenderloin on grid over medium-high heat; cover and grill turning frequently until internal temperature is 150°F., about 25 to 30 minutes. Cover and let stand 10 minutes before slicing.

In large bowl, combine salad greens and onion. Drizzle reserved vinaigrette over greens; toss until well mixed. Arrange salad on individual serving plates. Top with pork slices and raspberries.

Makes 4 servings

GREG'S GRILLING TIP

No matter how hungry you are and how good dinner smells, you'll want to cover cooked meat and let it rest at least 10 minutes before you dig in. The temperature of the meat will rise several degrees for perfect doneness, and the juices settle back into the meat. That keeps the meat moist and juicy, and it will be easier to slice.

---

technique savvy

Tender Juicy Pork

Today's pork is very lean, and the secret to making it tender is to cook it quickly. Pork is food safe when the center is still pink. Remove it from the heat when the internal temperature is 150°F., cover loosely with foil, and let stand 10 minutes. As it rests, the internal temperature will rise to 155°F. The pork will be tender, juicy, and perfectly cooked.

Per serving

Calories 248
Fat 8 g
Cholesterol 84 mg
Sodium 74 mg
Carbohydrate 13 g
Fiber 1 g

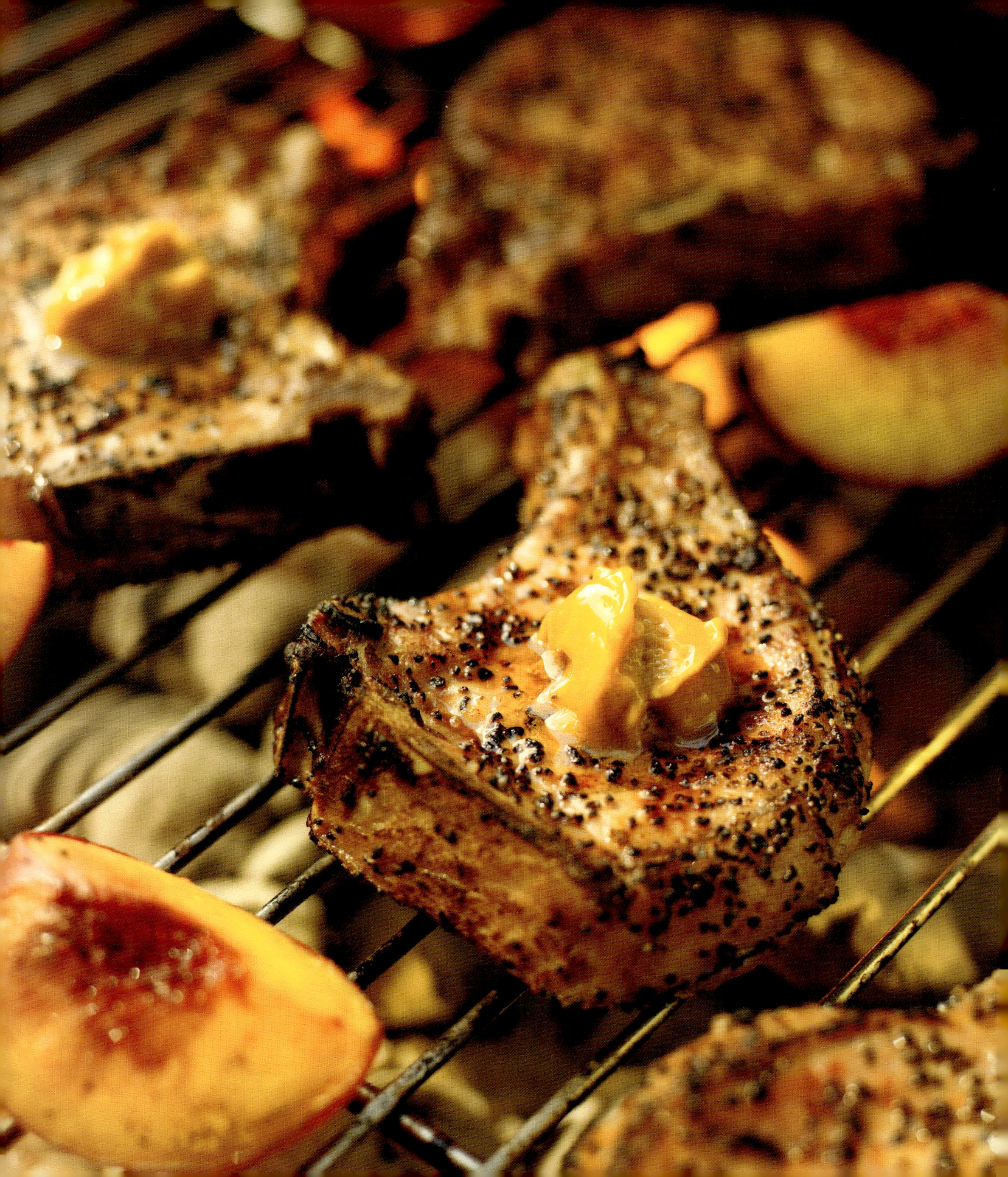

Whiskey Pepper Chops with Molasses Butter

Whiskey adds a hint of sweetness to these generously-cut chops. Try the Molasses Butter on dinner rolls, too!

4 bone-in rib pork chops,
  1 inch thick
  (about 1½ pounds)
Basic Brine (optional)
  (recipe on page 16)
¼ cup whiskey
2 tablespoons cracked black
  pepper
1½ teaspoons coarse salt
Molasses Butter

Trim and discard fat from chops. If desired, place chops in 2-gallon freezer-weight reclosable plastic bag; place bag in large bowl or baking dish. Pour brine over chops. Seal bag; refrigerate for 4 to 6 hours. Remove chops from brine and pat dry; discard brine.

Pour whiskey into shallow dish. In small bowl, combine pepper and salt (omit salt if chops are brined). Dip both sides of each chop in whiskey; coat evenly with pepper mixture. Place chops on oiled grid over medium-high heat; grill until well browned, about 1½ minutes per side. Move chops to side of grid for indirect heat (see *Indirect-Heat Grilling* on page 7); cover and grill until internal temperature is 150°F., about 5 to 6 minutes per side. Cover and let stand for 5 minutes. Serve with dollop of Molasses Butter.

Makes 4 servings

Molasses Butter

¼ cup butter, softened
1 tablespoon molasses
1 teaspoon fresh lemon juice

In small bowl with hand mixer, beat all ingredients at low speed until light and fluffy. Chill several hours or overnight to develop flavors.

Makes ¼ cup

Per 1 tablespoon Calories 122; Fat 12 g; Cholesterol 32 mg; Sodium 4 mg; Carbohydrate 4 g; Fiber 0 g

GREG'S GRILLING TIP
Give meat a chance to sear for at least 2 to 3 minutes, and it's much less likely to stick to the grate. So put the chops on the grill, put down the tongs, and leave them alone!

---

technique savvy

Compound Butters

Compound butters are back again and are terrific on steaks, chops, and just about anything else. Oh, and they're really easy to make, too.

Soften a stick of unsalted butter and season it with fresh herbs, garlic, spices, a tablespoon of wine or Worcestershire sauce – you name it. Beat the ingredients with an electric mixer until well combined.

Spoon the butter mixture evenly along one edge of a sheet of waxed paper and roll up to enclose the butter, forming a log. Twist the ends and chill for up to a week or freeze for up to a month. Then slice off a dab to top steaks, chops, fish, or vegetables for a delicious finishing touch.

Per serving with 1 tablespoon Molasses Butter

Calories 357
Fat 26 g
Cholesterol 97 mg
Sodium 752 mg
Carbohydrate 6 g
Fiber 1 g

Margarita Glazed Pork Chops

Sweet meets heat in this jalapeño jelly glaze spiked with tequila and lime. Dierbergs School of Cooking Manager Loretta Evans sets aside a little to serve as a sauce with the cooked chops.

4 boneless pork loin chops,
   ¾ inch thick
   (about 1¼ pounds)
Vegetable oil
Salt and pepper to taste
Margarita Glaze

Rub both sides of chops with vegetable oil and season with salt and pepper; set aside.

Remove half of the Glaze to baste chops; reserve remaining Glaze to serve as sauce. Place chops on oiled grid over medium-high heat; cover and grill turning and basting with Glaze until internal temperature is 150°F., about 4 to 5 minutes per side. Cover and let stand 5 minutes. Serve with reserved Margarita Glaze spooned over top.

Makes 4 servings

Margarita Glaze

⅔ cup jalapeño jelly
2 tablespoons tequila
2 teaspoons grated lime peel
1½ tablespoons lime juice
2 teaspoons minced fresh
   ginger root

Place jelly in 2-cup glass measure. Microwave (high) for 45 seconds or until melted. Stir in remaining ingredients. Store in refrigerator.

Makes ¾ cup

Per 2 tablespoons Calories 38; Fat 0 g; Cholesterol 0 mg; Sodium 4 mg; Carbohydrate 9 g; Fiber <1 g

VARIATION

Chili Cherry Chops Substitute Chili Cherry Sauce (recipe on page 12) for Margarita Glaze. Prepare chops according to directions above. Place chops on oiled grid over medium-high heat; cover and grill until browned on bottom side, about 4 minutes. Turn chops; spoon Chili Cherry Sauce over each chop. Reserve remaining Sauce to serve with pork. Grill until internal temperature is 150°F., about 4 to 5 minutes. Serve with reserved Chili Cherry Sauce.

Per serving Calories 365; Fat 9 g; Cholesterol 72 mg; Sodium 549 mg; Carbohydrate 39 g; Fiber 1 g

---

technique savvy
Fire Temperatures

Just like cooking indoors, different foods require different levels of heat on the grill. By holding your hand over the fire at grid height (about 5 inches above the fire), you can estimate how hot the fire is.

If you can hold you hand in place for…

2 seconds – the fire is hot

3 to 4 seconds – the fire is medium-hot

5 to 6 seconds – the fire is medium

7 seconds – the fire is medium-low

Per serving with 1 tablespoon Glaze

Calories 278
Fat 6 g
Cholesterol 60 mg
Sodium 56 mg
Carbohydrate 27 g
Fiber 1 g

DIERBERGS SCHOOL OF COOKING

Italian Sausage and Pasta Grill

Add zesty grilled sausage and vegetables to your pasta bowl for a quick and colorful entrée. Choose mild or hot Italian sausage to suit your taste.

6 Italian sausage links
1 cup dry red wine
Olive oil
3 medium zucchini, halved lengthwise
1 yellow bell pepper, quartered and seeded
1 package (16 ounces) penne pasta, cooked according to package directions
2 cups chopped tomato
2 tablespoons snipped fresh oregano, OR
2 teaspoons dried
Grated asiago or parmesan cheese

Pierce sausage links several times with fork. In medium saucepan, combine sausage and wine over medium-high heat; bring to a boil. Reduce heat and simmer for 10 minutes; drain well.

Place sausage links on oiled grid over medium-high heat; grill turning links often until golden brown and internal temperature is 155°F., about 12 to 15 minutes. Cover and let stand 10 minutes before slicing.

Brush zucchini and bell pepper with olive oil. Place vegetables on grid over medium-high heat; grill until vegetables are crisp-tender and lightly charred, about 3 to 5 minutes per side. Cut vegetables into 1-inch pieces.

In large bowl, combine sausage, grilled vegetables, pasta, tomato, and oregano; toss until well mixed. Serve with grated asiago cheese.

Makes 8 servings

GREG'S GRILLING TIP *For the easiest cleanup, use silicone basting brushes. They go right into the dishwasher.*

---

technique savvy

Wurst Comes to Wurst

Sausage is your link to a great meal from the grill in minutes. Fresh (uncooked) sausages come in all sorts of varieties, so there's something for every taste.

To speed up grilling time and add extra flavor, pierce sausage links several times with a fork. Then simmer bratwurst in beer or Italian sausage in dry red wine for about 10 minutes. Drain, place on grid, and grill over medium-high heat for about 10 minutes, or until internal temperature is 155°F.

If you skip the simmer step, place sausage links on grid over medium indirect heat (see *Indirect-Heat Grilling* on page 7) and grill turning occasionally for about 25 minutes.

Per serving

Calories 437
Fat 16 g
Cholesterol 46 mg
Sodium 387 mg
Carbohydrate 49 g
Fiber 3 g

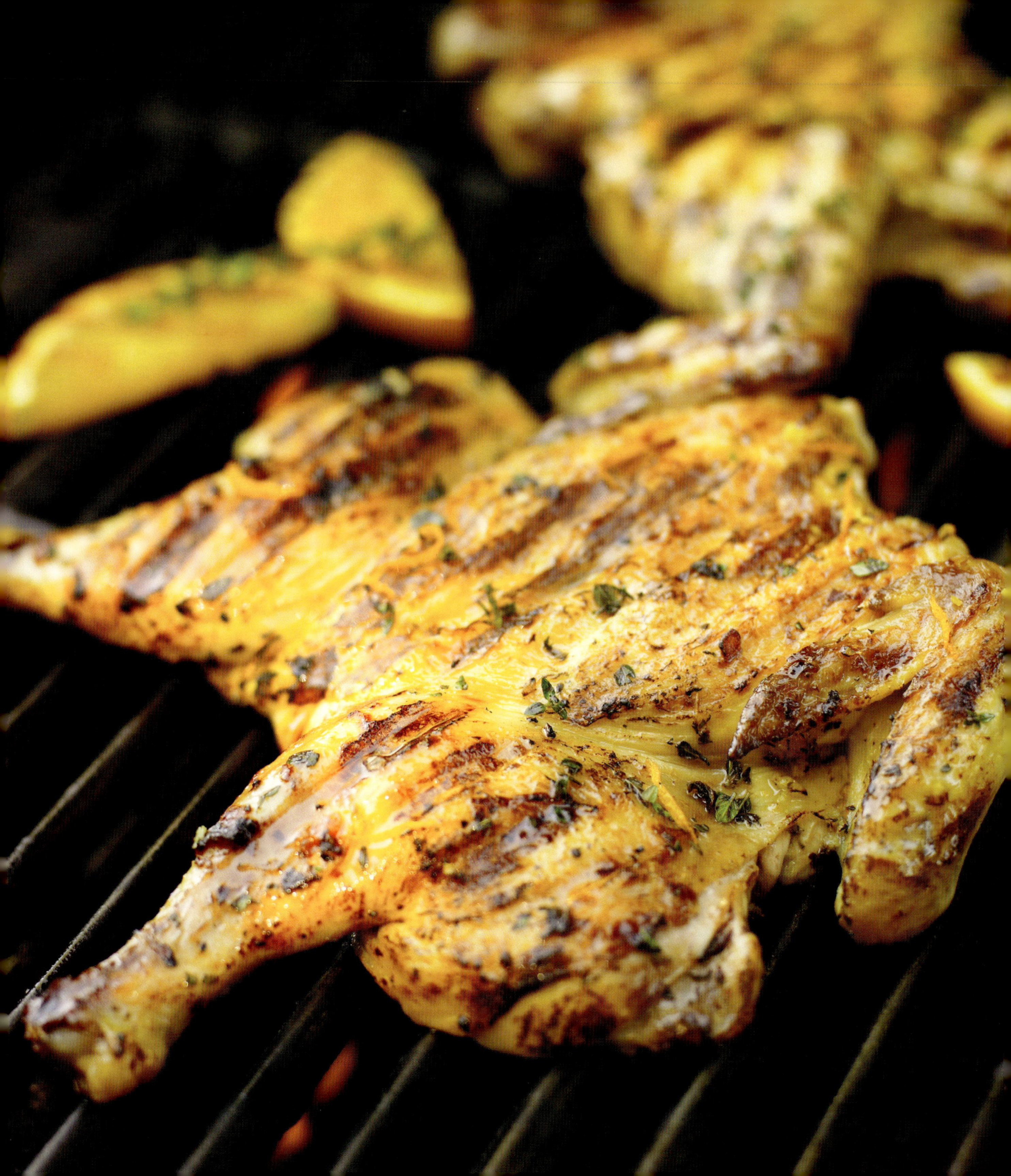

poultry, fish & seafood

Hens Under Bricks	42
Beer Can Chicken	43
Java BBQ Chicken	44
Tropical Spiced Chicken with Ginger Peach Salsa	44
Chicken with Lemon-Scented Tapenade	46
CLT Sandwich	47
Chicken Satay with Pineapple Chutney Glaze	49
Mediterranean Chicken Pizza	50
Apricot-Glazed Turkey Tenderloins	51
Bacon-Wrapped Turkey Medallions	51
Mojo Shrimp Salad	53
Salmon on a Plank	54
Teriyaki Grilled Salmon	54
Tuna Salade Niçoise with French Vinaigrette	56
Balsamic Fish Steaks with Artichoke Aïoli	58
Herbed Tilapia with Citrus Butter	59

◀ *Hens Under Bricks*
Recipe on page 42

technique savvy

Step-by-Step Instructions

Per 3-ounce cooked portion (without skin)

Calories 140
Fat 6 g
Cholesterol 90 mg
Sodium 78 mg
Carbohydrate 1 g
Fiber 0 g

Hens Under Bricks

According to Dierbergs School of Cooking Manager Ginger Gall, weighting down the hens with bricks helps them cook quickly, keeps them moist and juicy inside, and makes them crispy on the outside.

2 frozen Cornish hens (about 1½ pounds each), thawed
½ cup olive oil
¼ cup white balsamic or white wine vinegar
1 tablespoon grated orange peel
¼ cup fresh orange juice
4 teaspoons minced fresh ginger root
4 teaspoons snipped fresh thyme
½ teaspoon coarse salt
½ teaspoon freshly ground black pepper

Remove and discard giblets from hen cavities. Place hens breast-side down on large cutting board. **1** Using kitchen shears, cut along one side of the backbone from tail to neck end. Pull open hen halves; be careful not to tear skin. Cut down other side of backbone; remove and discard backbone. Place hens breast-side up, and with heel of hands, press down firmly on hens to flatten.

Place hens in large freezer-weight reclosable plastic bag. In 2-cup glass measure, combine remaining ingredients. Pour over hens; seal bag and turn to coat meat. Place bag on plate and marinate in refrigerator for several hours or overnight. Remove hens from bag; discard marinade.

Lightly coat underneath side of jellyroll pan with no-stick cooking spray. Place hens skin-side down on oiled grid over medium-high indirect heat (see *Indirect-Heat Grilling* on page 7). Set jellyroll pan on top of hens and weight down pan with 2 foil-wrapped bricks; cover and grill for 5 minutes. **2** Using heavy pot holders, carefully remove jellyroll pan and bricks; rotate hens. Replace jellyroll pan and bricks; cover and grill for 5 minutes. Using heavy pot holders, carefully remove jellyroll pan and bricks; turn hens over. Replace bricks and jellyroll pan; cover and grill until internal temperature is 165°F., about 10 minutes. Cover and let stand 10 minutes. Cut each hen in half along breastbone.

Makes 4 servings

TIP Sometimes called *game hens*, these miniature chickens make a lovely presentation for a special meal. Cornish hens are available frozen and range from 1 to 2 pounds. For hens weighing 1 pound, plan on 1 hen per person. For larger hens, plan on ½ hen per person.

Beer Can Chicken

You'll never taste a juicer chicken! The beer steams the inside of the bird, and all the juices are trapped in its crispy skin.

1 whole chicken
  (4 to 5 pounds)
1 to 2 tablespoons lemon
  pepper seasoning
1 can (12 to 16 ounces) beer

Remove and discard giblets from chicken cavity. Use fingers to gently separate skin from breast meat. Rub lemon pepper under skin, over outside, and in cavity of bird.

Open beer can; remove half the beer. Place beer can on cutting board. Slide chicken over beer can so chicken stands upright. (The drumsticks and beer can form a tripod to steady the chicken.) **1** Place chicken on grid over medium-high indirect heat (see *Indirect-Heat Grilling* on page 7); cover and grill until internal temperature of breast meat is 165°F., about 1 to 1¼ hours.

2 Carefully remove chicken and can from grill; be careful not to spill beer. Cover and let stand 10 minutes before lifting chicken off of beer can. Cut into serving-size pieces.

Makes 4 servings

GREG'S GRILLING TIP

It's a little tricky to get the chicken off the grill. Try using several paper towels in each hand to grasp the chicken and can to lift it onto a cutting board.

technique savvy

Step-by-Step Instructions

Per 3-ounce cooked portion (without skin)

Calories 142
Fat 6 g
Cholesterol 64 mg
Sodium 267 mg
Carbohydrate 0 g
Fiber 0 g

Java BBQ Chicken

Coffee infuses the chicken with deep, rich flavor. A splash of coffee liqueur makes the sauce sweet, sticky, and fun!

Per serving

Calories 142
Fat 1 g
Cholesterol 43 mg
Sodium 762 mg
Carbohydrate 14 g
Fiber 0 g

3/4 cup chili sauce
3 tablespoons brown sugar
2 tablespoons coffee-flavored liqueur (Kahlúa, Starbucks, or Tia Maria)
1 clove garlic, minced
1/2 teaspoon hot pepper sauce
6 boneless, skinless chicken breast halves (about 1½ pounds), pounded to even thickness

In small saucepan, combine chili sauce, brown sugar, liqueur, garlic, and hot pepper sauce over medium-high heat; bring to a boil. Reduce heat and simmer stirring frequently until slightly thickened, about 5 minutes.

Place chicken on oiled grid over medium-high heat; cover and grill turning and basting occasionally with sauce until internal temperature is 165°F., about 4 to 5 minutes per side.

Makes 6 servings

TIP For really juicy chicken, use the Java Brine (recipe on page 16) before cooking.

Tropical Spiced Chicken with Ginger Peach Salsa

What a great combination of flavors! You'll get rave reviews every time you serve it, but don't tell anybody how easy it is to prepare.

Per serving

Calories 128
Fat 2 g
Cholesterol 43 mg
Sodium 230 mg
Carbohydrate 13 g
Fiber 1 g

4 boneless, skinless chicken breast halves (about 1 pound), pounded to even thickness
Pickapeppa Glaze (recipe on page 13)
Ginger Peach Salsa (recipe on page 63)

Place chicken in shallow dish; pour Glaze over chicken, turning to coat each piece. Place chicken on oiled grid over medium-high heat; cover and grill until internal temperature is 165°F., about 4 to 5 minutes per side. Serve with Ginger Peach Salsa spooned over top.

Makes 4 servings

TIP For really juicy chicken, use the Basic Brine (recipe on page 16) before cooking.

44 DIERBERGS SCHOOL OF COOKING

Tropical Spiced Chicken with Ginger Peach Salsa

Chicken with Lemon-Scented Tapenade

This is the perfect party dish! It's easy to make with big, bold flavors that will have everyone talking.

ingredient savvy

How Much Chicken

Bigger is Better seems to apply to everything these days. But super-sized ingredients can affect the outcome of a recipe as well as your waistline.

The *right* portion size for meat, poultry, and fish recommended by USDA and the American Heart Association is 4 ounces uncooked – about the size of a computer mouse. Most recipes for boneless, skinless chicken breast halves are formulated with that in mind.

When the chicken breast halves that you buy are exceptionally large, simply cut them in half to make each into two portions.

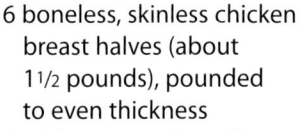

Per serving

Calories 151
Fat 8 g
Cholesterol 43 mg
Sodium 318 mg
Carbohydrate 2 g
Fiber <1 g

---

6 boneless, skinless chicken breast halves (about 1½ pounds), pounded to even thickness
3 tablespoons olive oil
1 tablespoon grated lemon peel
3 tablespoons fresh lemon juice
¼ cup snipped fresh mint
½ teaspoon salt
½ teaspoon ground black pepper
Lemon-Scented Tapenade
Fresh mint (optional)

Lemon-Scented Tapenade

1 large clove garlic
1 jar (3 ounces) pitted green olives, drained
1 jar (3 ounces) pitted ripe olives, drained
¼ cup fresh parsley leaves
¼ cup sliced green onion
2 tablespoons fresh lemon juice
2 tablespoons olive oil

Place chicken in large freezer-weight reclosable plastic bag. In 1-cup glass measure, combine olive oil, lemon peel and juice, mint, salt, and pepper. Pour over chicken; seal bag and turn to coat chicken. Place bag on plate and marinate in refrigerator for 30 minutes. Remove chicken from bag; discard marinade.

Place chicken on grid over medium-high heat; cover and grill until internal temperature is 165°F., about 4 to 5 minutes per side. Serve with Lemon-Scented Tapenade spooned over top. If desired, garnish with mint.

Makes 6 servings

Fit food processor with steel knife blade. With machine running, drop garlic through feed tube; process until finely chopped. Add olives, parsley, green onion, and lemon juice; process until chopped. With machine running, pour olive oil through feed tube in slow, steady stream. Chill several hours or overnight to develop flavors. Serve over grilled chicken or fish.

Makes about 1 cup

TIP Spoon Tapenade over cream cheese and serve with French bread slices for a impromptu appetizer.

Per 2 tablespoons Calories 64; Fat 7 g; Cholesterol 0 mg; Sodium 261 mg; Carbohydrate 2 g; Fiber <1 g

CLT Sandwich

Inspired by the bacon-centric original, this grilled chicken sandwich is simple and satisfying.

4 boneless, skinless chicken breast halves (about 1 pound), pounded to even thickness
¼ cup fresh lemon juice
¼ cup drained oil-packed sun-dried tomatoes with herbs, reserving oil
2 teaspoons Italian herb seasoning
1 clove garlic, minced
½ cup mayonnaise
1 loaf (8 ounces) Dierbergs French baguette, cut into 4 pieces and split
Olive oil no-stick cooking spray
4 lettuce leaves
4 tomato slices

Place chicken in large freezer-weight reclosable plastic bag. In 1-cup glass measure, stir together lemon juice, 2 tablespoons of the sun-dried tomato oil, Italian seasoning, and garlic. Pour over chicken; seal bag and turn to coat chicken. Place bag on plate and marinate in refrigerator for several hours or overnight. Remove chicken from bag; discard marinade.

Finely chop sun-dried tomatoes. In small bowl, stir together mayonnaise and sun-dried tomatoes. Cover and chill at least 30 minutes or overnight to develop flavors.

Place chicken on grid over medium-high heat; cover and grill until internal temperature is 165°F., about 4 to 5 minutes per side.

Lightly coat cut-sides of bread with cooking spray. Place cut-side down on grid over medium-high heat; grill until lightly toasted and grill marks appear, about 1 to 2 minutes. Spread mayonnaise mixture on grilled sides of bread. Layer lettuce, tomatoes, and grilled chicken on half of the bread slices; top with remaining bread slices.

Makes 4 servings

EAT HEARTY TIP Use light mayonnaise and spread only 1 tablespoon mayonnaise mixture on each sandwich.

Per serving Calories 318; Fat 9 g; Cholesterol 48 mg; Sodium 510 mg; Carbohydrate 36 g; Fiber 2 g

GREG'S GRILLING TIP

If you like this sandwich, try substituting a grilled salmon fillet for the chicken. It's always a hit at our house!

technique savvy

Pounding Chicken Breasts

Many recipes call for boneless, skinless chicken breasts pounded to an even thickness. To keep counters and utensils clean as you pound, slip chicken breasts one at a time into a large freezer-weight plastic bag. Close but do not seal. Gently pound them with the smooth side of a meat mallet to the desired thickness. This helps them cook more quickly and evenly, so watch cooking times carefully.

Per serving

Calories 498
Fat 28 g
Cholesterol 53 mg
Sodium 541 mg
Carbohydrate 38 g
Fiber 1 g

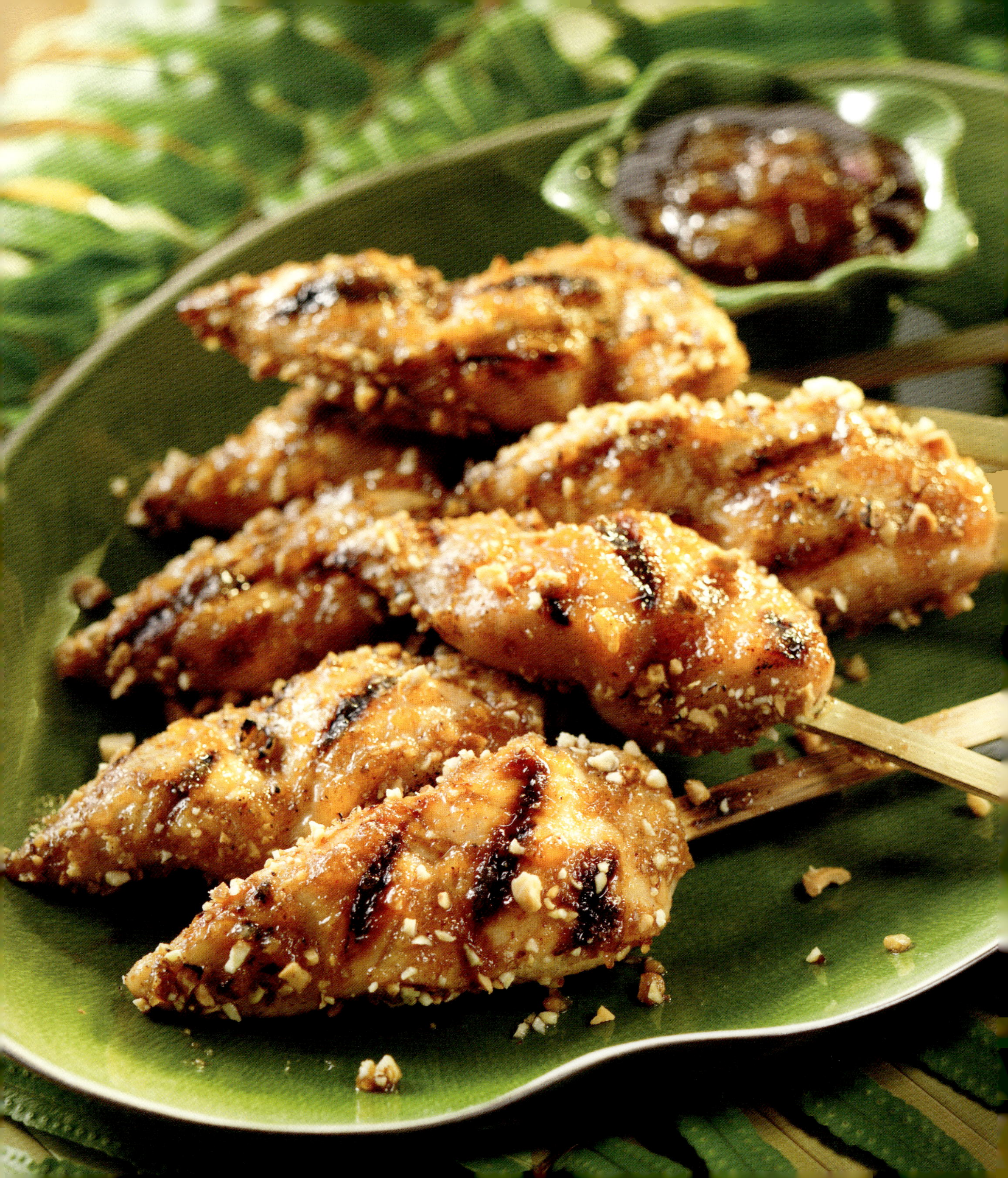

Chicken Satay with Pineapple Chutney Glaze

Dierbergs Prepared Foods Manager and former School of Cooking Manager Pam Pahl bastes these savory skewers with a tangy pineapple glaze. Roll them in chopped macadamia nuts for a crunchy finishing touch.

1 pound chicken tenders
Pineapple Chutney Glaze
Wooden skewers, soaked in water for 30 minutes
1 cup macadamia mixed nuts, cashews, or peanuts, toasted and finely chopped

If desired, remove tendons from chicken. Grasp tendon with paper towel. Use kitchen shears to scrape meat away from tendon. Place chicken in large freezer-weight reclosable plastic bag. Pour 1/2 cup of the Glaze over chicken; reserve remaining Glaze for dipping sauce. Seal bag and turn to coat chicken. Place bag on plate and marinate in refrigerator for 2 to 4 hours. Remove chicken from bag; discard marinade.

Weave chicken onto skewers. Place skewers on oiled grid over medium-high heat; cover and grill until browned, about 4 to 5 minutes per side.

Place nuts in glass pie plate. Brush chicken with reserved Glaze. Roll each skewer in chopped nuts. Serve with remaining Pineapple Chutney Glaze.

Makes 4 servings

Pineapple Chutney Glaze

1 jar (12 ounces) pineapple preserves
2 shallots, finely chopped
1 tablespoon white balsamic or white wine vinegar
1/2 teaspoon chipotle chile powder
1/2 teaspoon ground allspice
1/2 teaspoon salt

In work bowl of food processor fitted with steel knife blade, combine all ingredients; pulse several times. Store in refrigerator.

Makes about 1 1/2 cups

Per 2 tablespoons Calories 89; Fat <1 g; Cholesterol 0 mg; Sodium 119 mg; Carbohydrate 23 g; Fiber <1 g

GREG'S GRILLING TIP
It's important to soak wooden skewers, but the ends can still burn on the grill. After you thread the food on, wrap the exposed ends of the skewers in foil to avoid charred sticks.

cuisine savvy

What is Satay?

Whether you spell it satay or sate (sah-TAY), these tasty little skewers have come a long way from simple Indonesian street fare. Start with strips of marinated chicken, meat, or firm fish like salmon or tuna, and weave them onto skewers. Then grill them until they're browned and cooked through.

Satay is traditionally served with a spicy peanut dipping sauce, but you can get creative here with other lively flavors. Small skewers make a nice appetizer from the grill, or make larger skewers and serve them over rice as an entrée.

Per serving

Calories 425
Fat 17 g
Cholesterol 43 mg
Sodium 342 mg
Carbohydrate 47 g
Fiber 1 g

Mediterranean Chicken Pizza

Pizza on the grill? Why not! Grilling gives the crust – and the toppings – a slightly smoky flavor that's a great change of pace.

1½ pounds Roma tomatoes
⅓ cup shredded fresh basil
1 tablespoon snipped fresh oregano
2 cloves garlic, minced
1 tablespoon olive oil
1 tablespoon balsamic vinegar
1 teaspoon fresh lemon juice
Cornmeal Pizza Crust
1 package (6 to 10 ounces) cooked chicken strips
1 can (2.25 ounces) sliced kalamata olives, drained
2 ounces (½ cup) crumbled feta cheese
Salt and pepper to taste

Cut tomatoes into ¼-inch-thick slices; place on large platter. In 1-cup measure, stir together basil, oregano, garlic, olive oil, vinegar, and lemon juice; drizzle over tomatoes, turning tomatoes to coat both sides. Marinate at room temperature for at least 30 minutes or up to 2 hours to develop flavors.

Mix Pizza dough according to directions. Shape dough and grill on first side as directed. Drain tomatoes; arrange over partially baked crust. Top with chicken, olives, and feta. Sprinkle lightly with salt and generously with pepper. Slide onto oiled grid; cover and grill until crust is lightly browned on bottom, about 3 to 4 minutes.

Makes 6-8 servings

Cornmeal Pizza Crust

1¾ cups flour
¼ cup cornmeal
1 envelope (2¼ teaspoons) fast-rising dry yeast
½ teaspoon salt
⅔ cup warm (110° to 115°F.) water
1 tablespoon olive oil
1 tablespoon honey

Place flour, cornmeal, yeast, and salt in work bowl of food processor fitted with steel knife blade. In 1-cup glass measure, stir together warm water, olive oil, and honey. With machine running, pour liquid mixture through feed tube in slow, steady stream; process until dough forms a ball and cleans sides of bowl. Process for 30 seconds. Let dough rest in processor bowl for 10 minutes.

Dust pizza pan with cornmeal. Shape dough into rough 12-inch circle; place on prepared pizza pan. Slide crust onto oiled grid over medium-high heat; grill until lightly browned on bottom, about 3 to 4 minutes. Turn crust over onto pizza pan. Add toppings as desired. Slide onto oiled grid; cover and grill until crust is lightly browned on bottom, about 3 to 4 minutes.

Makes one 12-inch pizza crust

Per ⅙ crust Calories 190; Fat 3 g; Cholesterol 0 mg; Sodium 196 mg; Carbohydrate 38 g; Fiber 1 g

---

technique savvy
Covering the Grill

To capture the great smoky flavor that grilling is all about, keep the cover on when cooking over the coals. This allows the heat to circulate evenly and prevents flare-ups.

Per serving

Calories 227
Fat 7 g
Cholesterol 18 mg
Sodium 493 mg
Carbohydrate 32 g
Fiber 2 g

Apricot-Glazed Turkey Tenderloins

You're only four ingredients and minutes away from a delicious grilled entrée. Need we say more?

2 turkey tenderloins (about 1½ to 2 pounds)
1 tablespoon olive oil
1 tablespoon grill seasoning blend
⅓ cup apricot preserves, melted

Rub tenderloins with olive oil; sprinkle with seasoning. Place turkey on grid over medium-high heat; cover and grill turning frequently until internal temperature is 165°F., about 20 minutes. Brush with preserves during last 5 minutes of grilling time. Cover and let stand 5 minutes before slicing.

Makes 6-8 servings

Per serving

Calories 121
Fat 2 g
Cholesterol 42 mg
Sodium 285 mg
Carbohydrate 9 g
Fiber 0 g

Bacon-Wrapped Turkey Medallions

Why wait till Thanksgiving? Turkey is terrific any time, especially sizzling hot off the grill.

½ pound pepper crusted bacon
2 turkey tenderloins (about 1½ to 2 pounds)
3 tablespoons brown sugar
Chili Cherry Sauce (recipe on page 12) OR Dierbergs Kitchen Signature Bourbon Sauce

Place bacon slices on paper towel-lined microwave-safe plate. Cover with paper towels and microwave (high) for 2 to 3 minutes until partially cooked.

Slice turkey tenderloins into 8 medallions; flatten slightly with heel of hand. Place brown sugar on sheet of waxed paper. Roll edge of medallions in brown sugar. Wrap bacon around medallions; secure with wooden picks.

Place medallions on oiled grid over medium-high heat; grill for 1½ minutes per side. Move medallions to side of grid for indirect heat (see *Indirect-Heat Grilling* on page 7); cover and grill until internal temperature is 165°F., about 8 to 10 minutes per side. Brush with Sauce during last 2 to 3 minutes of grilling time.

Makes 6-8 servings

Per serving

Calories 269
Fat 8 g
Cholesterol 55 mg
Sodium 487 mg
Carbohydrate 25 g
Fiber <1 g

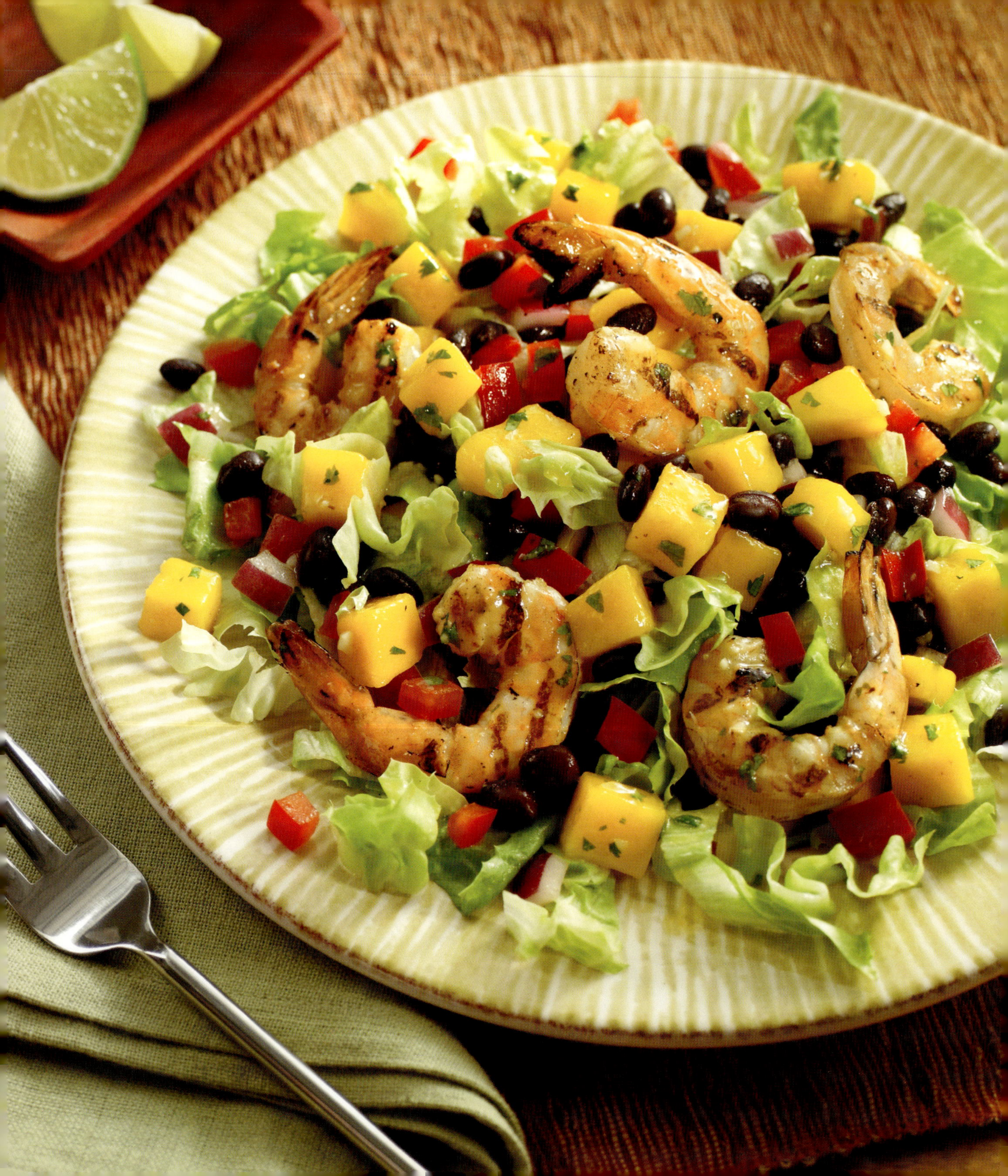

Mojo Shrimp Salad

Mojo (MO-ho) sauce, a blend of citrus, garlic, oil, and herbs, is the Caribbean way to brighten any dish. Try this with grilled chicken or pork, too!

1½ pounds large (26 to 30 count) shrimp, peeled and deveined
Mojo Marinade (divided) (recipe on page 14)
1 mango, pitted and chopped (see *Step-by-Step Instructions* on page 32)
1 can (15 ounces) black beans, rinsed and drained
½ cup diced red bell pepper
¼ cup diced red onion
Wooden skewers, soaked in water for 30 minutes
1 bag (8 ounces) shredded iceberg lettuce

Place shrimp in large freezer-weight reclosable plastic bag. Pour ¼ cup Marinade over shrimp; seal bag and turn to coat shrimp. Place bag on plate and marinate in refrigerator for 30 minutes. Remove shrimp from marinade; discard marinade.

In large bowl, combine mango, beans, bell pepper, and onion. Stir in remaining Marinade. Chill.

1 Thread shrimp in "C" shape onto skewers. **2** If desired, slide second skewer into shrimp parallel to first skewer to prevent shrimp from twirling. Place skewers on grid over medium-high heat; grill until shrimp are opaque throughout, about 2 to 3 minutes per side.

Divide lettuce among 6 individual serving plates. Top with mango mixture and grilled shrimp.

Makes 6 servings

VARIATION

Gingered Shrimp Salad Substitute Ginger Marinade (recipe on page 14) for the Mojo Marinade.

Per serving Calories 221; Fat 4 g; Cholesterol 140 mg; Sodium 876 mg; Carbohydrate 20 g; Fiber 6 g

GREG'S GRILLING TIP

Garlic is good stuff, but the aroma is hard to get off of your hands. Rub your hands on something made of stainless steel – like a spoon – and the garlic odor will disappear.

---

technique savvy

Step-by-Step Instructions

Per serving

Calories 283
Fat 10 g
Cholesterol 140 mg
Sodium 478 mg
Carbohydrate 25 g
Fiber 6 g

DIERBERGS SCHOOL OF COOKING

Salmon on a Plank

Brush salmon fillets with a lively herb and mustard glaze. It's simple, elegant, and ready in minutes.

Per serving
Calories 159
Fat 9 g
Cholesterol 50 mg
Sodium 140 mg
Carbohydrate 1 g
Fiber 0 g

1 (15-inch) cedar grilling plank, soaked in water for at least 1 hour
1 salmon fillet (about 1½ to 2 pounds)
Olive oil
Coarse salt and fresh ground black pepper to taste
2 tablespoons Dijon mustard
1 tablespoon snipped fresh tarragon or rosemary

Place soaked plank on grid over medium-high heat; cover and heat for 3 minutes. Turn plank over; cover and heat until light smoke develops, about 3 minutes. Brush flesh side of salmon with olive oil; season with salt and pepper. In small bowl, combine mustard and tarragon. Brush over salmon; place skin-side down on heated plank over medium-high heat; cover and grill until internal temperature is 145°F., about 15 to 20 minutes. Transfer salmon to serving plate; remove plank from grill.

Makes 6-8 servings

TIP See *Plank Cooking* on page 7.

Teriyaki Grilled Salmon

As food stylist for Dierbergs Presents Everybody Cooks® TV show and School of Cooking instructor, Carol Ziemann pairs teriyaki sauce with rich salmon for a perfect match.

Per serving
Calories 335
Fat 17 g
Cholesterol 66 mg
Sodium 835 mg
Carbohydrate 19 g
Fiber <1 g

½ cup reduced-sodium soy sauce
¼ cup dry sherry
2 teaspoons cornstarch
⅓ cup honey
1 tablespoon minced fresh ginger root
1 teaspoon grated lime peel
1 tablespoon fresh lime juice
2 tablespoons vegetable oil
1 salmon fillet (about 1½ to 2 pounds), cut into 6 strips
Black and red pepper blend (optional)

In small saucepan, combine soy sauce, sherry, and cornstarch; stir until cornstarch is dissolved. Cook stirring constantly over medium-high heat until sauce thickens. Remove from heat; stir in honey, ginger, and lime peel and juice. Remove ¼ cup sauce for basting salmon; reserve remaining sauce to serve with grilled salmon. In small bowl, stir 1 to 2 teaspoons of the basting sauce into the vegetable oil; brush over salmon. Sprinkle with pepper blend.

Place salmon flesh-side down on oiled grid over medium-high heat; cover and grill for 4 minutes. Place sheet of heavy-duty foil on grid; turn salmon skin-side down on top of foil. Brush basting sauce over salmon; cover and grill until opaque throughout and internal temperature is 145°F., about 4 to 5 minutes. Slide metal spatula between flesh and skin. (Skin will stick to foil; discard foil.) Place salmon on serving plate; serve with reserved sauce.

Makes 6 servings

Salmon on a Plank ▸

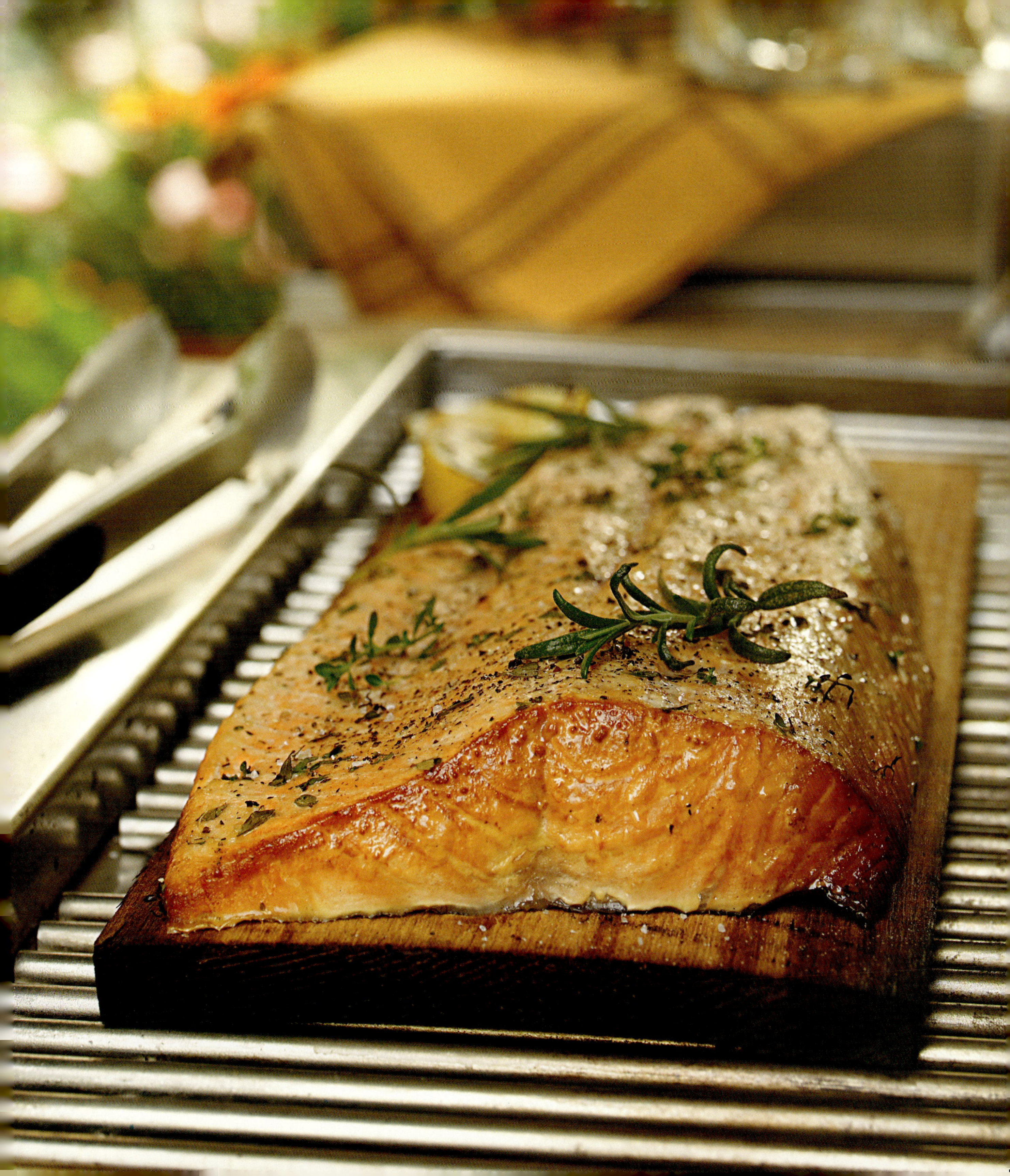

Tuna Salade Niçoise with French Vinaigrette

In the French Riviera city of Nice, many dishes include ripe olives and tomatoes. Our version of classic Salade Niçoise (nee SWAHZ) features tuna steaks, grilled to perfection.

technique savvy
Grilling Tuna

Fresh tuna has a rich, meaty texture and is cooked to perfection when the flesh turns opaque but is still pink in the center. Like any cut of meat, tuna is very dry when it is overcooked. For best results, cook fresh tuna until the internal temperature is 145°F.

1 pound tuna steaks
French Vinaigrette (divided)
1 bag (10 ounces) spring mix salad greens
1 head Boston lettuce, leaves separated, rinsed, and drained
1 bag (12 ounces) fresh green beans, cooked according to package directions and immediately dipped in ice water to stop cooking
2 vine-ripened tomatoes, cut into wedges
2 hard-cooked eggs, cut into wedges
1 can (2.25 ounces) sliced kalamata or ripe olives, drained
1 tablespoons capers, rinsed and drained

Place tuna in shallow dish. Pour 1/4 cup of the Vinaigrette over tuna; reserve remaining Vinaigrette for salad. Cover and marinate in refrigerator for 30 minutes. Remove tuna from marinade; discard marinade.

Place tuna on grid over medium-high heat; cover and grill until internal temperature is 145°F., about 4 to 5 minutes per side. Do not overcook. Let stand 5 minutes before slicing.

Place salad greens in large bowl. Drizzle reserved Vinaigrette over greens; toss until well mixed. Line 4 individual dinner plates with Boston lettuce leaves; top with salad greens. Arrange sliced tuna, green beans, tomatoes, and eggs on each salad. Sprinkle olives and capers over tops.

Makes 4 servings

French Vinaigrette

1/4 cup white wine vinegar
1 teaspoon sugar
1/2 teaspoon salt
1/2 teaspoon dried basil
1/4 teaspoon dry mustard
1/4 teaspoon ground black pepper
1/3 cup olive oil

In small bowl, whisk together all ingredients except olive oil. Whisking vigorously, add oil in slow, steady stream until well blended.

Makes about 2/3 cup

Per 2 tablespoons Calories 135; Fat 14 g; Cholesterol 0 mg; Sodium 234 mg; Carbohydrate 1 g; Fiber <1 g

Per serving

Calories 302
Fat 16 g
Cholesterol 144 mg
Sodium 365 mg
Carbohydrate 13 g
Fiber 6 g

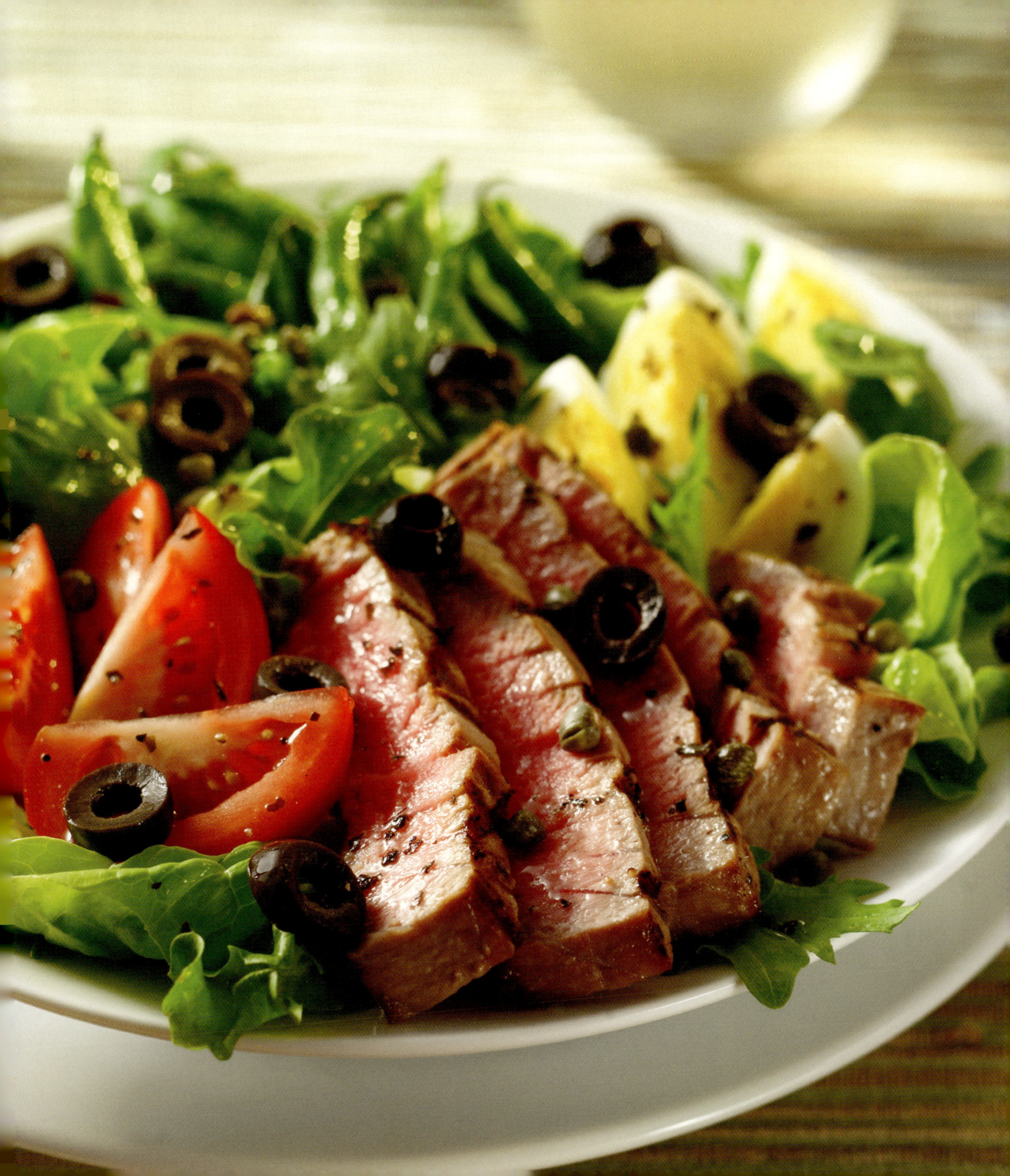

Balsamic Fish Steaks with Artichoke Aïoli

Fresh tuna has a firm, meaty texture that makes it ideal for grilling. Dierbergs Staff Culinary Professional Therese Lewis gets rave reviews for this fantastic sauce.

4 tuna or salmon steaks (about 1 pound)
1 tablespoon brown sugar
2 tablespoons balsamic vinegar
1 tablespoon olive oil
1 tablespoon snipped fresh basil
Freshly ground black pepper

Place tuna in shallow dish. In 1-cup glass measure, stir together brown sugar, vinegar, oil, and basil; pour over fish. Cover and marinate in refrigerator for 30 minutes. Remove fish from marinade; discard marinade.

Season fish with pepper. Place on oiled grid over medium-high heat; cover and grill until internal temperature is 145°F., about 4 to 5 minutes per side. Do not overcook. Serve with Artichoke Aïoli.

Makes 4 servings

Artichoke Aïoli

1 can (14 ounces) artichoke hearts, drained and coarsely chopped
¾ cup light mayonnaise
¼ cup light dairy sour cream
1 clove garlic, minced
2 tablespoons fresh lemon juice
2 tablespoons capers, rinsed and drained
1 tablespoon snipped fresh basil

In medium bowl, stir together all ingredients. Cover and chill at least 30 minutes or overnight to develop flavors.

Makes about 3 cups

TIP The recipe makes a generous amount and leftovers taste even better the next day. Spoon Aïoli over steamed green beans or broccoli for a quick vegetable sauce. Or stir it into cooked, drained spinach. Put a dollop of Aïoli on French bread slices and broil for 1 to 2 minutes or until bubbly for a quick appetizer. Toss halved, grilled, roasted, or boiled baby potatoes with Aïoli for an easy gourmet potato salad.

Per 2 tablespoons Calories 35; Fat 3 g; Cholesterol 3 mg; Sodium 143 mg; Carbohydrate 2 g; Fiber 0 g

---

technique savvy
Out of Gas

You've been thinking all day about something wonderful for dinner tonight, hot off the grill. You certainly don't want to run out of fuel before you're done cooking! If your gas grill doesn't have a fuel gauge, try this trick. Bring one or two cups of water to a boil and pour it over the side of the fuel tank. Where the tank feels hot, it's empty. Where it still feels cool, there's propane in the tank.

Per serving with 2 tablespoons Aïoli

Calories 162
Fat 4 g
Cholesterol 54 mg
Sodium 186 mg
Carbohydrate 3 g
Fiber 0 g

Herbed Tilapia with Citrus Butter

Choose fillets that are at least 4 ounces each to ensure proper grilling. Serve them topped with a savory butter for a simple yet sophisticated supper.

4 fresh tilapia fillets
 (about 1 pound)
Lemon pepper seasoning
Citrus Butter or Dierbergs
 Kitchen Signature
 Chardonnay Herb Butter

Season both sides of tilapia with lemon pepper. Place on oiled grid over medium-high heat; cover and grill until fish flakes easily with fork and internal temperature is 145°F., about 10 minutes per inch of thickness. To serve, top each fillet with dollop of Citrus Butter.

Makes 4 servings

Citrus Butter

1/4 cup butter, softened
3 tablespoons snipped fresh
 herbs (basil, dill, chives)
1 teaspoon grated lemon
 peel

In small bowl, stir together all ingredients. Chill several hours or overnight to develop flavors.

Makes 1/3 cup

Per 1 tablespoon Calories 82; Fat 9 g; Cholesterol 24 mg; Sodium 1 mg; Carbohydrate <1 g; Fiber <1 g

GREG'S GRILLING TIP

Fish is a healthy and satisfying entrée, and it gets a great smoky flavor when you cook it on the grill. And a great bonus for grilling fish – any fishy aromas stay outdoors!

---

technique savvy

Grilling Fish

Fish is great on the grill! It cooks quickly, so be ready to serve up a meal in minutes with these helpful hints.

• Firm fish like salmon, tuna, halibut, and swordfish have intense flavor, a firm texture, and are well-suited for grilling.

• White fish like tilapia and cod have a milder flavor and more delicate flesh. Thicker fillets will cook more evenly and hold their shape better on the grill.

• Liberally brush the grid or wire basket with oil before putting fish on the grill.

• Measure fish at its thickest part and cook it 10 minutes per inch of thickness. Fish is done when the internal temperature is 145°F.

**Per serving with
1 tablespoon Citrus Butter**

Calories 125
Fat 10 g
Cholesterol 47 mg
Sodium 25 mg
Carbohydrate <1 g
Fiber <1 g

DIERBERGS SCHOOL OF COOKING

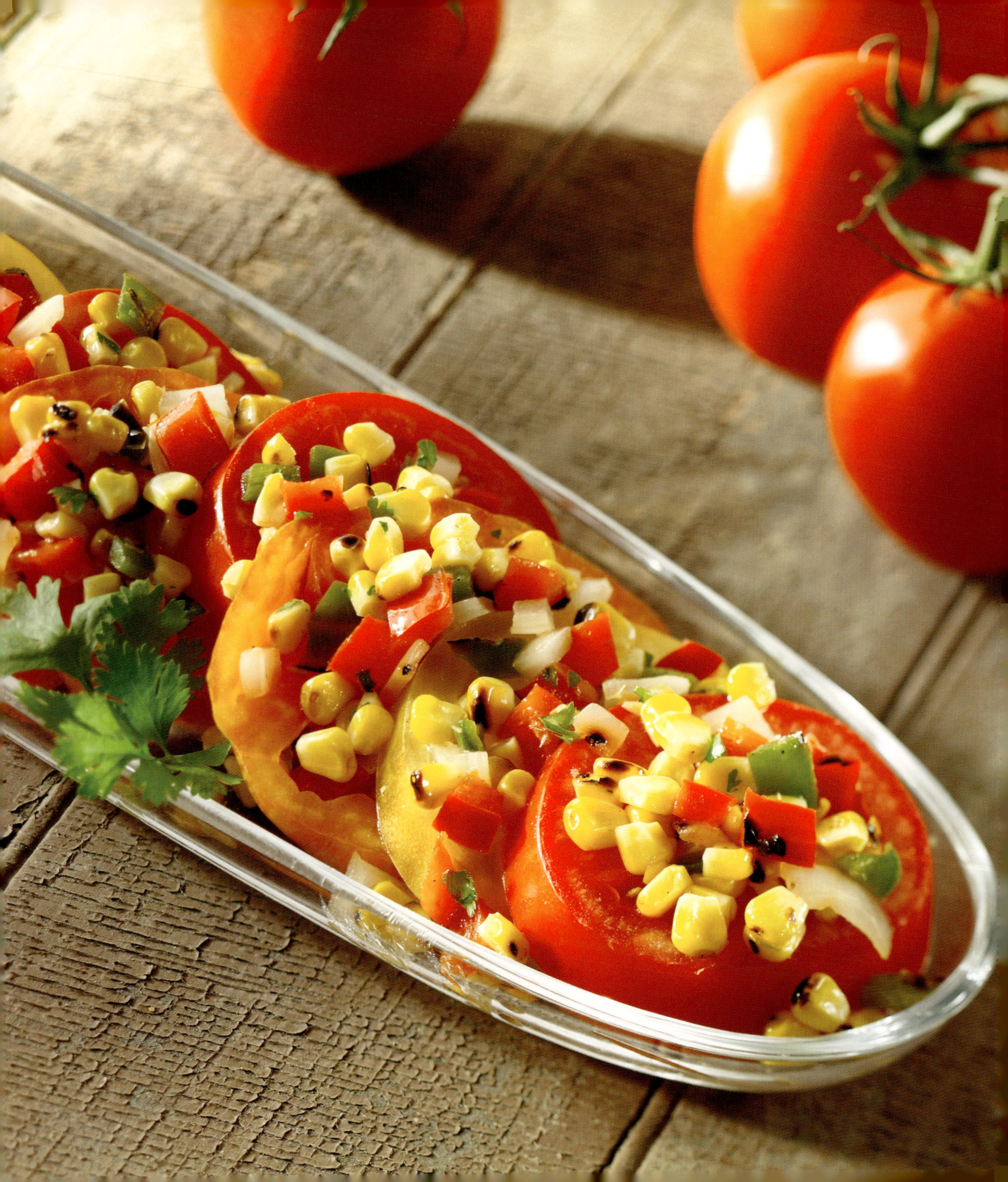

sides & meatless

Grilled Corn Salsa	62
Fresh Tomato Salsa	62
Fresh Fruit Salsa	63
Grilled Baby Potato and Green Bean Salad	64
Southwest Potato Salad	65
Herbed Tomato Mozzarella Salad	67
Greek Cucumber Salad	68
Southwest Chopped Salad	69
Minty Melon Salad	70
Asian Slaw	72
Mango and Lime Slaw	72
Tuscan Grilled Vegetables	73
Bella on a Bun	74
Asparagus with Lemon Dijon Sauce	75
Summer Vegetables with Bowtie Pasta	77
Smoky Grilled Quesadillas	78
Rosemary Garlic Bread	79
Grilled Bruschetta	79
Blushing Sangria	81
Paradise Coolers	81

◄ *Grilled Corn Salsa*
Recipe on page 62

Grilled Corn Salsa

This colorful salsa is a fiesta of summer flavors. It's the perfect way to dress up almost any grilled meat or fish. Serve over tomatoes for a wonderful summer salad. It's a terrific dip for chips, too!

Per 2 tablespoons
Calories 20
Fat 1 g
Cholesterol 0 mg
Sodium 2 mg
Carbohydrate 3 g
Fiber <1 g

Olive oil
3 ears corn-on-the-cob, tassels and husks removed
1 red bell pepper, quartered and seeded
2 to 3 jalapeños, halved, seeded, and deveined
1 medium onion, cut into wedges from top to root, leaving root intact
2 tablespoons olive oil
1 tablespoon honey
1 tablespoon fresh lime juice
1 tablespoon snipped fresh cilantro or parsley
Salt and pepper to taste

Brush corn, bell pepper, jalapeños, and onion with olive oil. Place vegetables on grid over medium heat; cover and grill turning occasionally until crisp-tender and lightly charred, about 6 to 10 minutes. Cool slightly.

Cut kernels from cob with serrated knife (see *Step-by-Step Instructions* on page 65). Finely chop jalapeños; chop bell pepper and onion.

In medium bowl, combine grilled vegetables. Stir in the 2 tablespoons olive oil, honey, lime juice, and cilantro. Season with salt and pepper. Let stand 15 minutes to develop flavors. Serve chilled or at room temperature.

Makes about 4 cups

Fresh Tomato Salsa

Everyone needs a good tomato salsa in their recipe repertoire. Look no further! This one is mild enough for everyone's taste and goes great with everything from your favorite Mexican dishes to a basket of crunchy chips.

Per 2 tablespoons
Calories 21
Fat 2 g
Cholesterol 0 mg
Sodium 49 mg
Carbohydrate 2 g
Fiber 0 g

1 pint grape or cherry tomatoes, quartered
1/4 cup minced shallot
2 tablespoons snipped fresh cilantro or parsley
1 clove garlic, minced
3 tablespoons extra virgin olive oil
2 tablespoons white balsamic or white wine vinegar
1/2 teaspoon salt
Coarsely ground black pepper to taste

In medium bowl, combine all ingredients; stir to combine. Let stand 15 minutes to develop flavors.

Makes about 3 cups

Fresh Fruit Salsa

The combination of fresh fruit, peppers, and a splash of citrus goes perfectly with grilled chicken, pork, fish, or seafood. Try all of our delicious variations.

- 2 cups chopped fresh fruit
- 1/2 cup finely chopped red onion
- 1/2 cup finely chopped red bell pepper
- 1 jalapeño, halved, seeded, deveined, and finely diced (optional)
- 2 tablespoons snipped fresh cilantro, parsley, or mint
- 1 teaspoon grated fresh lime, lemon, or orange peel
- 2 tablespoons fresh lime, lemon, or orange juice
- 1 tablespoon olive oil
- 1 teaspoon honey

In medium bowl, combine all ingredients; stir to combine. Cover and chill for 2 to 4 hours to develop flavors.

Makes 2¼ cups

VARIATIONS

Ginger Peach Salsa Use 2 cups chopped peaches, cilantro, and lime peel and juice. Add 1 teaspoon minced fresh ginger root. (See *Tropical Spiced Chicken with Ginger Peach Salsa* photo on page 45.)

Per 2 tablespoons Calories 41; Fat 1 g; Cholesterol 0 mg; Sodium 1 mg; Carbohydrate 8 g; Fiber 1 g

Tropical Fruit Salsa Use 1 cup chopped mango, 1 cup chopped papaya, cilantro, and lemon peel and juice. Add 1/3 cup chopped macadamia nuts (optional) and 2 teaspoons minced fresh ginger root.

Per 2 tablespoons Calories 22; Fat 1 g; Cholesterol 0 mg; Sodium 1 mg; Carbohydrate 4 g; Fiber 1 g

Strawberry Salsa Use 2 cups coarsely chopped strawberries, mint, and orange peel and juice.

Per 2 tablespoons Calories 16; Fat 1 g; Cholesterol 0 mg; Sodium 1 mg; Carbohydrate 2 g; Fiber 1 g

Watermelon Salsa Use 2 cups chopped and drained watermelon, mint, lime peel and juice, and 1/4 teaspoon coarse salt.

Per 2 tablespoons Calories 16; Fat 1 g; Cholesterol 0 mg; Sodium 27 mg; Carbohydrate 3 g; Fiber <1 g

---

ingredient savvy

Fresh Chiles

Whether they're mild or wild, fresh chiles have a subtle fruitiness of their own and add a colorful kick to fruit salsas.

Generally, the smaller the chile and the more pointed the tip, the hotter the variety. Fresh poblanos, also known as green chiles, are very mild. Jalapeños range from hot to very hot. And habañeros are among the hottest of all.

The oils in peppers can sting eyes and skin, so handle them with care. Wear disposable gloves when seeding fresh chiles, or immediately wash your hands to prevent irritation.

Per serving

Calories 24
Fat 1 g
Cholesterol 0 mg
Sodium 1 mg
Carbohydrate 5 g
Fiber 1 g

technique savvy
Foiled Again!

Cook more than just the entrée on the grill. Wrap vegetables in foil packets and cook right alongside the meat.

Tear off a large sheet of heavy-duty foil or smaller sheets for individual portions. Arrange veggies and their seasonings on foil. Bring sides of foil to center in series of locked folds; fold up ends to seal completely allowing a little room for steam to expand.

Place packet on grid and grill turning occasionally until desired doneness. Enjoy the delicious veggies with no cleanup!

Per serving
Calories 243
Fat 13 g
Cholesterol 0 mg
Sodium 167 mg
Carbohydrate 31 g
Fiber 5 g

Grilled Baby Potato and Green Bean Salad

Potato salad from the grill? Why not! Ours has tender green beans, rich kalamata olives, and a tangy balsamic vinaigrette for a delicious change of pace.

1 bag (28 ounces) baby red potatoes, quartered
4 tablespoons extra virgin olive oil (divided)
1 pound fresh green beans, trimmed and halved
½ cup chopped shallot
½ cup pitted kalamata or ripe olives, halved
¼ cup snipped fresh basil
2 tablespoons balsamic vinegar
1 tablespoon Dijon mustard
2 to 3 cloves garlic, minced
Salt and pepper to taste

Place potatoes in single layer on large sheet of heavy-duty foil; drizzle with 1 tablespoon of the olive oil. Place green beans on top in even layer. Bring sides of foil to center in series of locked folds; fold up ends to seal completely. Place packet, potato-side down, on grid over medium-high heat; cover and grill until packet puffs slightly and potatoes are tender, about 15 to 20 minutes. (Do not turn packet.)

Place potatoes and green beans in serving bowl; add shallot, olives, and basil. In small bowl, whisk together vinegar, mustard, and garlic. Whisking vigorously, add remaining 3 tablespoons olive oil in slow, steady stream. Drizzle over vegetables; toss until well mixed. Season with salt and pepper. Serve warm or at room temperature.

Makes 6 servings

GREG'S GRILLING TIP *Instead of making a packet out of foil, try using foil grilling bags. You can pick them up next to the foils and wraps at Dierbergs. It's a really easy way to cook, and there's nothing to cleanup!*

Southwest Potato Salad

Grilling the corn and potatoes adds a smoky flavor to this venerable barbecue side dish. Add a creamy, chile-spiked dressing to bring all of the flavors together.

6 ears corn-on-the-cob, tassels and husks removed
4 medium red potatoes (about 1 pound), quartered lengthwise
Olive oil
2 teaspoons chili powder (divided)
1 cup mayonnaise
1 tablespoon fresh lime juice
1 can (2.25 ounces) sliced ripe olives, drained
1 jalapeño, halved, seeded, deveined, and finely chopped
1/3 cup snipped fresh cilantro or parsley
Salt and pepper to taste

Brush corn and potatoes with olive oil. Sprinkle 1/2 teaspoon of the chili powder over corn. Place corn and potatoes on oiled grid over medium-high heat; cover and grill turning occasionally until tender and lightly charred, about 6 to 10 minutes for corn and 20 minutes for potatoes. Cool slightly.

1 Cut kernels from cob with serrated knife. Cut potatoes into bite-size pieces.

In large bowl, stir together mayonnaise, lime juice, and remaining 1 1/2 teaspoons chili powder. Stir in corn, potatoes, olives, jalapeño, and cilantro. Season with salt and pepper. Serve warm or at room temperature.

Makes 8-10 servings

GREG'S GRILLING TIP

No-stick cooking sprays are as handy at the grill as they are in the kitchen. Look for one made just for grilling – it will hold up better at high cooking temperatures. For safety, follow the directions on the can and spray it only on the grid, tongs, or pan – never on hot surfaces or directly over an open flame.

technique savvy

Step-by-Step Instructions

Per serving

Calories 249
Fat 19 g
Cholesterol 8 mg
Sodium 192 mg
Carbohydrate 19 g
Fiber 3 g

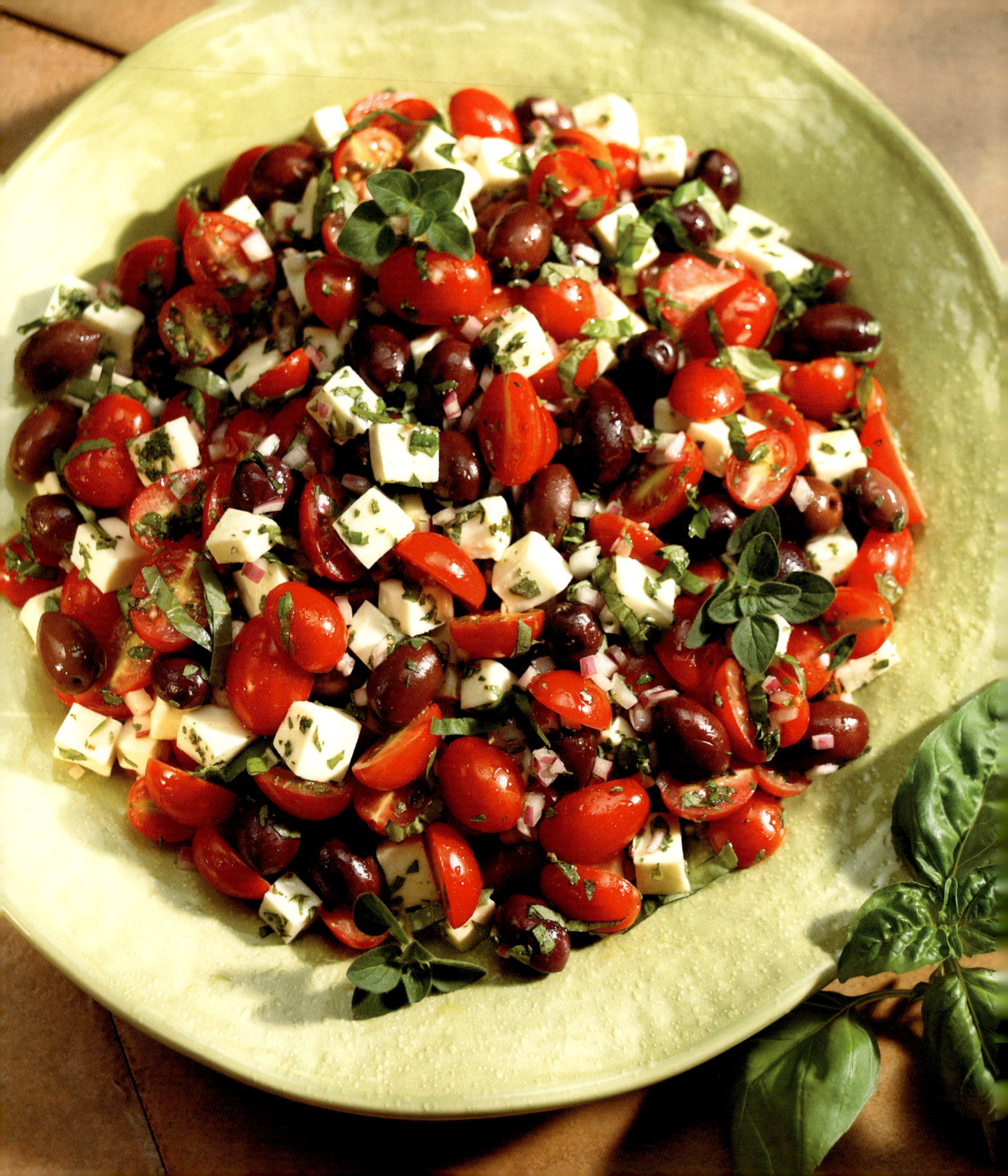

Herbed Tomato Mozzarella Salad

A fistful of fragrant herbs turns a medley of sweet tomatoes, salty olives, and creamy mozzarella into a flavorful salad. Serve it as bruschetta on top of crusty bread for a colorful appetizer.

- 1 pint grape or cherry tomatoes, halved
- 8 ounces fresh mozzarella, cubed
- 1 cup pitted kalamata or ripe olives, drained
- ½ cup chopped red onion
- 3 tablespoons white balsamic or white wine vinegar
- 2 tablespoons extra virgin olive oil
- 2 tablespoons snipped fresh basil
- 2 tablespoons snipped fresh oregano
- Coarse salt and freshly ground black pepper to taste

In medium bowl, combine all ingredients; stir to combine. Chill for 1 to 2 hours to develop flavors. Serve chilled or at room temperature.

Makes 4-6 servings

VARIATION

Greek Herbed Tomato Salad Omit mozzarella, red onion, vinegar, and basil. Add ½ cup crumbled feta cheese and 1 tablespoon fresh lemon juice. If desired, slice olives. (See *Petite Tenders with Greek Herbed Tomato Salad* photo on page 25.)

Per serving Calories 148; Fat 14 g; Cholesterol 7 mg; Sodium 313 mg; Carbohydrate 6 g; Fiber <1 g

---

ingredient savvy

Fresh Herbs

Store most fresh herbs by standing the bunch in a glass with about an inch of cold water. Secure a plastic bag over the top and refrigerate for up to ten days, changing the water every two days.

Rinse herbs in cool water just before using and drain on paper towels.

Add fresh herbs at the end of the recipe cooking time to preserve their bright flavor. Add dried herbs at the beginning of cooking to release their flavor.

Use three times the amount of chopped fresh herbs in place of dried herbs called for in a recipe. For example, use 1 tablespoon (3 teaspoons) chopped fresh basil instead of 1 teaspoon dried.

Per serving

Calories 121
Fat 9 g
Cholesterol 8 mg
Sodium 200 mg
Carbohydrate 8 g
Fiber 1 g

Greek Cucumber Salad

Cool, crisp cucumbers topped with a tangy yogurt and feta dressing make a refreshing summer salad. Serve it alongside grilled chicken or fish.

3 cups peeled, seeded, and thinly sliced cucumbers (about 1 to 1½ pounds)
½ cup chopped red bell pepper
⅓ cup thinly slivered red onion
4 ounces (1 cup) crumbled feta cheese
⅔ cup plain low-fat yogurt or dairy sour cream
1 clove garlic, minced
1 teaspoon snipped fresh dill weed, OR ½ teaspoon dried
1 teaspoon snipped fresh oregano, OR ½ teaspoon dried
Salt and pepper to taste

In large bowl, combine cucumbers, bell pepper, and onion. In small bowl, stir together feta, yogurt, garlic, dill, and oregano. Pour over vegetables; gently toss until well mixed. Season with salt and pepper. Chill to develop flavors. Serve within 6 hours.

Makes 6 servings

TIP If desired, baby cucumbers can be used in place of regular cucumbers. There's no need to peel or seed, just slice and enjoy them.

---

technique savvy

Cucumbers

It is generally not necessary to peel a cucumber. You can rake it lengthwise with fork tines for a decorative pattern. Or if the skin is waxy, you can remove it with a vegetable peeler.

Removing seeds from the cucumber makes it more enjoyable to eat, and will help prevent a soggy dish. Cut the cucumber in half lengthwise. Then use a small spoon or melon ball cutter to scrape out the seeds.

Per serving

Calories 84
Fat 4 g
Cholesterol 13 mg
Sodium 234 mg
Carbohydrate 7 g
Fiber 1 g

Southwest Chopped Salad

This colorful and hearty salad is a wonderful meatless entrée, and if you add grilled chicken or beef – YUM! Kids will love the lightly-spiced taco ranch dressing!

- 1/3 cup light ranch dressing
- 1 tablespoon reduced-sodium taco seasoning
- 1/2 teaspoon hot pepper sauce
- 1 ear corn-on-the-cob, OR 1/2 cup frozen corn, thawed and drained
- 1 head romaine lettuce, chopped (about 8 cups)
- 1 can (15 ounces) black beans, rinsed and drained
- 1/4 cup chopped red onion
- 4 ounces (1 cup) shredded 2% milk colby-monterey jack cheese blend
- 1 large tomato, chopped
- Tortilla chips (plain or flavored)

In small bowl, stir together ranch dressing, taco seasoning, and hot pepper sauce; set aside.

Remove tassel and dark outer husks from corn, leaving remaining husks intact. Microwave (high) for 2 minutes; let stand for several minutes. Remove husks and silk from corn. Cut kernels from cob with serrated knife (see *Step-by-Step Instructions* on page 65).

In large bowl, combine lettuce, beans, corn, onion, cheese, and tomato. Drizzle dressing over salad; toss until well mixed. Serve with tortilla chips.

Makes 4-6 servings

GREG'S GRILLING TIP

If you light the grill to cook an entrée, go ahead and grill the corn, too (see Grilled Vegetable Time Table *on page 73). It will add a lot of extra flavor to your salad.*

---

technique savvy

Crisping Greens

For crisp salads, wash and dry greens in a salad spinner. Roll them gently in paper towels and chill for several hours. For longer storage, place in a plastic bag and chill. Greens will stay fresh for five to seven days.

Per serving without chips

Calories 187
Fat 7 g
Cholesterol 14 mg
Sodium 564 mg
Carbohydrate 20 g
Fiber 7 g

technique savvy

Step-by-Step Instructions

Minty Melon Salad

Three cheers for this light and refreshing combination of luscious summer fruits. A drizzle of minty syrup adds just a hint of sweetness.

1 cup fresh mint leaves
1 cup sugar
1 cup water
8 cups watermelon balls or cubes
4 cups honeydew balls or cubes
2 cups fresh blueberries
Mint sprigs (optional)

In medium saucepan, combine mint and sugar. [1] Using muddler or back of wooden spoon, mash mint leaves with sugar until [2] leaves are bruised. Stir in water; bring to a boil, stirring occasionally, over medium-high heat. Reduce heat; simmer for 5 minutes without stirring. Remove from heat and steep for 10 minutes; strain. Chill. (Syrup may be refrigerated for up to 2 weeks.)

Combine fruit in large bowl. Drizzle syrup over top; toss until well mixed. Chill for 30 minutes to develop flavors. If desired, garnish with additional mint sprigs.

Makes 12 servings

Per serving

Calories 127
Fat <1 g
Cholesterol 0 mg
Sodium 12 mg
Carbohydrate 33 g
Fiber 2 g

DIERBERGS SCHOOL OF COOKING

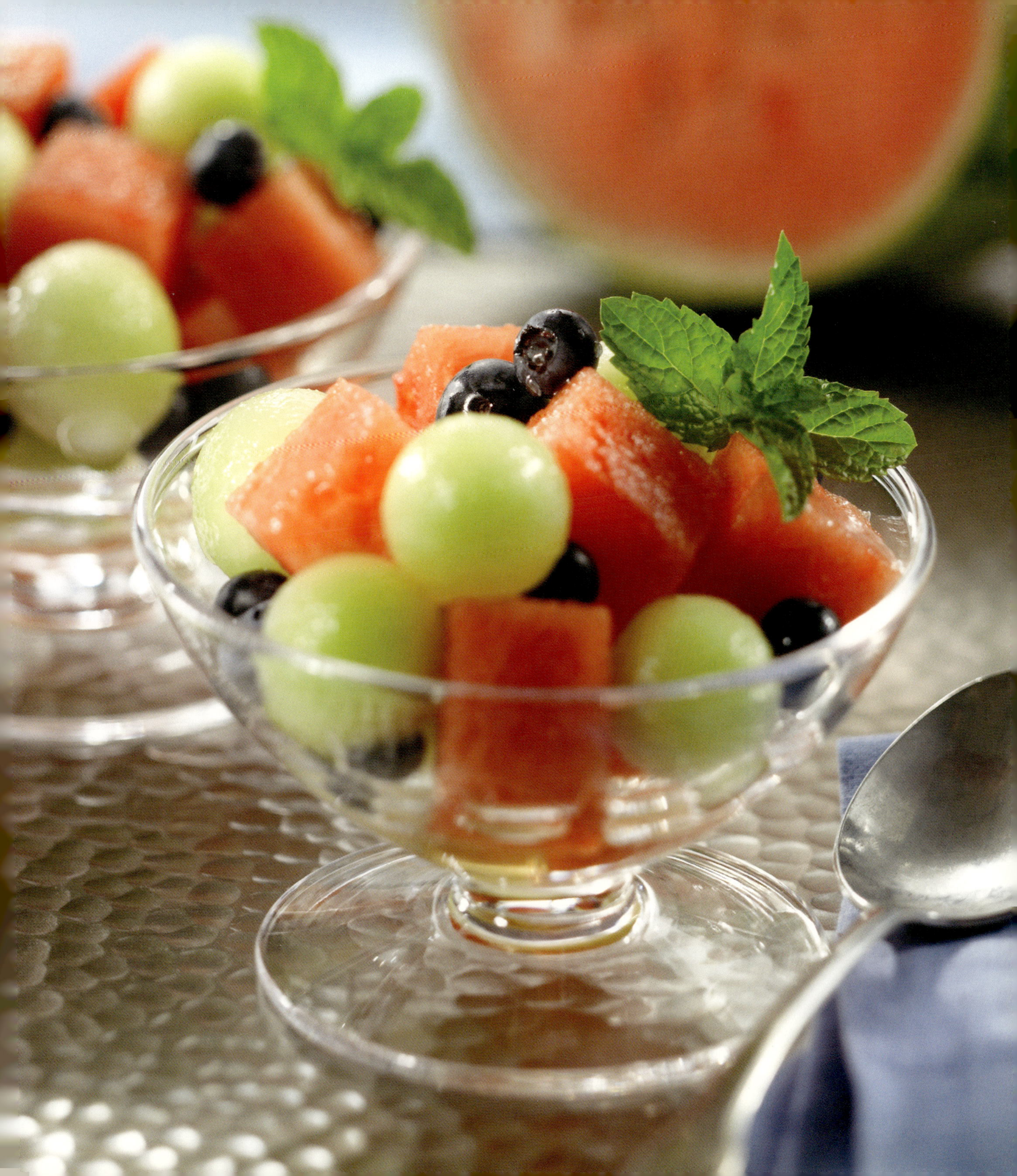

Asian Slaw

Napa cabbage is crunchy yet a little more tender than regular cabbage. The light, creamy dressing has a hint of soy sauce and cilantro.

Per serving

Calories 67
Fat 5 g
Cholesterol 5 mg
Sodium 199 mg
Carbohydrate 4 g
Fiber 1 g

- 8 cups thinly sliced napa cabbage (about 1 pound)
- 1 red bell pepper, quartered, seeded, and diced
- ½ cup thinly sliced green onion (tops only)
- ½ cup light mayonnaise
- 2 tablespoons chopped fresh cilantro or parsley
- 2 tablespoons rice or white wine vinegar
- 1 tablespoon light soy sauce

In large bowl, combine cabbage, bell pepper, and green onion. In small bowl, stir together mayonnaise, cilantro, vinegar, and soy sauce. Pour over cabbage; toss until well mixed.

Makes 8 servings

Mango and Lime Slaw

Looking for something a little different to take along to your next backyard get-together? Dierbergs Test Kitchen Manager Karen Hurych loves this cool, refreshing slaw with island flavors.

Per serving

Calories 73
Fat 4 g
Cholesterol 0 mg
Sodium 54 mg
Carbohydrate 11 g
Fiber 2 g

- 1 package (16 ounces) cole slaw mix
- 1 mango, pitted and chopped (see *Step-by-Step Instructions* on page 32)
- ¼ cup finely chopped red onion
- 1 teaspoon grated lime peel
- 3 tablespoons fresh lime juice
- 2 tablespoons extra virgin olive oil
- 1 tablespoon honey
- 1 teaspoon Cajun/Creole seasoning
- 1 teaspoon Dijon mustard

In large bowl, combine slaw mix, mango, and onion. In small bowl, stir together lime peel and juice, olive oil, honey, seasoning, and mustard. Pour over cabbage; toss until well mixed.

Makes 6-8 servings

TIP Try using 3-color cole slaw mix or angel slaw mix.

Grilled Vegetable Time Table

Prepare vegetables as directed below, brush with olive oil or marinade, and season as desired. Grill turning occasionally and brushing with olive oil until vegetables are crisp-tender and lightly charred.

Grill for 6 to 8 minutes	Preparation
Asparagus	Snap off white ends; place diagonally on oiled grid
Bell Pepper	Quarter and seed
Button Mushrooms	Thread onto skewers
Carrots	Peel; place diagonally on oiled grid
Zucchini or Summer Squash	Trim; halve lengthwise

Grill for 8 to 10 minutes	Preparation
Corn-on-the-Cob	Remove tassels and husks
Eggplant	Peel; cut 1/2 inch thick
Onion	Peel; halve through root end
Potatoes	Cut into wedges

Tuscan Grilled Vegetables

Grilling the lemon halves makes them especially juicy while adding a colorful, rustic garnish for the vegetables.

1 package (8 ounces) button mushrooms
2 small zucchini (about 1 pound), sliced 1/2 inch thick
Wooden skewers, soaked in water for 30 minutes
2 small lemons, halved
1/2 recipe Tuscan Marinade (recipe on page 15)

Thread vegetables onto skewers; brush vegetables and cut-side of lemons with Marinade. Place skewers on grid over medium-high heat; cover and grill turning occasionally and brushing with Marinade until vegetables are crisp-tender and lightly charred, about 6 to 10 minutes. Place lemons cut-side down on grid; grill until lightly charred and grill marks appear, about 2 to 3 minutes.

To serve, squeeze grilled lemons over vegetables.

Makes 4 servings

---

technique savvy

Grilling Vegetables

Most vegetables do well with medium-high heat. If you are using very dense, thick vegetables, you may want to use a slightly lower temperature.

Brushing the vegetables with oil will add flavor and keep the vegetables moist and tender. If they start to look dry as they cook, just brush them again with oil.

A simple seasoning of salt and pepper is all you need, but you can be creative with marinades and basting sauces for even more flavor.

Turn vegetables with tongs as they cook; forks can easily tear the vegetables.

Don't be afraid of a little charring. The dark grill marks will give the vegetables a delicious, smoky flavor.

Per serving

Calories 73
Fat 5 g
Cholesterol 0 mg
Sodium 159 mg
Carbohydrate 8 g
Fiber 2 g

Bella on a Bun

It doesn't get more versatile than a meaty portabella mushroom cooked on the grill. Serve it as is for a meatless burger, or slice the caps to top pizza, bruschetta, or a thick, juicy steak.

technique savvy
Step-by-Step Instructions

6 portabella mushrooms
¼ cup extra virgin olive oil
1 tablespoon balsamic vinegar
1 teaspoon garam masala (optional)
4 cloves garlic, minced (divided)
6 slices onion (Maui, Vidalia, red), sliced ½ inch thick
Olive oil
Salt and pepper to taste
¼ cup mayonnaise
3 tablespoons chutney (Major Grey's or pear cardamom)
6 slices provolone cheese
3 tablespoons butter, softened
6 sandwich buns, split

1 Remove and discard stems and gills from mushrooms. Place mushrooms in large freezer-weight reclosable plastic bag. In 1-cup glass measure, combine oil, vinegar, garam masala, and 3 cloves minced garlic. Pour over mushrooms; seal bag and turn to coat mushrooms. Place on plate and marinate in refrigerator overnight. Remove mushrooms from bag; discard marinade.

Brush onion slices with olive oil; season with salt and pepper. Place onion on grid over medium-high heat; grill turning once for 15 to 20 minutes.

In small bowl, stir together mayonnaise and chutney; set aside.

Place mushrooms on oiled grid; grill for 3 to 4 minutes per side. Place 1 slice cheese on top of each mushroom; grill until cheese is melted, about 1 to 2 minutes.

Combine butter with remaining 1 clove minced garlic; spread on bun halves. Place buns cut-side down on oiled grid; grill until lightly toasted and grill marks appear, about 1 to 2 minutes. Spread mayonnaise mixture over grilled side of buns.

Place 1 mushroom on bottom side of buns; top each with grilled onion slice and top of buns.

Makes 6 sandwiches

TIP Garam masala is an Indian spice blend that adds spicy heat. Look for it in the spice aisle at Dierbergs.

Per serving with 2 teaspoons mayonnaise mixture

Calories 338
Fat 19 g
Cholesterol 43 mg
Sodium 383 mg
Carbohydrate 32 g
Fiber 1 g

Asparagus with Lemon Dijon Sauce

If you haven't grilled asparagus, what are you waiting for? Dierbergs School of Cooking Manager Sally Bruns adds lemon, soy sauce, and Dijon to these smoky spears.

1½ pounds asparagus
2 tablespoons olive oil (divided)
3 tablespoons fresh lemon juice
1 tablespoon soy sauce
1 tablespoon Dijon mustard
1 clove garlic, minced
2 teaspoons brown sugar
Coarse salt and freshly ground black pepper to taste

Snap off and discard tough white ends from asparagus. Place asparagus spears on platter. Drizzle 1 tablespoon of the olive oil over top; toss to coat. Place diagonally on grid over medium-high heat; grill turning occasionally until crisp-tender and slightly charred, about 5 to 7 minutes.

Place asparagus on serving plate. In small bowl, stir together the remaining 1 tablespoon of olive oil, lemon juice, soy sauce, mustard, and brown sugar; drizzle over asparagus. Season with salt and pepper.

Makes 8 servings

GREG'S GRILLING TIP

Grilling is the best way to cook asparagus. You can't beat the smoky flavor. Either put the spears diagonally right onto the grid, or you can put them in a grill basket so they don't slip through the grate.

ingredient savvy

Fresh Asparagus

Always choose firm, bright green asparagus with tightly closed purple-tinted buds. Asparagus can be stored for one to two days in the refrigerator. Stand the bunch upright in a container with about an inch of water, cover the tops with a plastic bag, and refrigerate.

Just before cooking, gently snap each stalk at the bottom. It will break at the very spot where woodiness begins. Rinse with water, pat dry, and toss with a tablespoon or two of olive oil before placing on the grill. Grilling caramelizes the natural sugars in asparagus and gives the spears a sweet, smoky flavor.

Per serving

Calories 48
Fat 3 g
Cholesterol 0 mg
Sodium 162 mg
Carbohydrate 4 g
Fiber 1 g

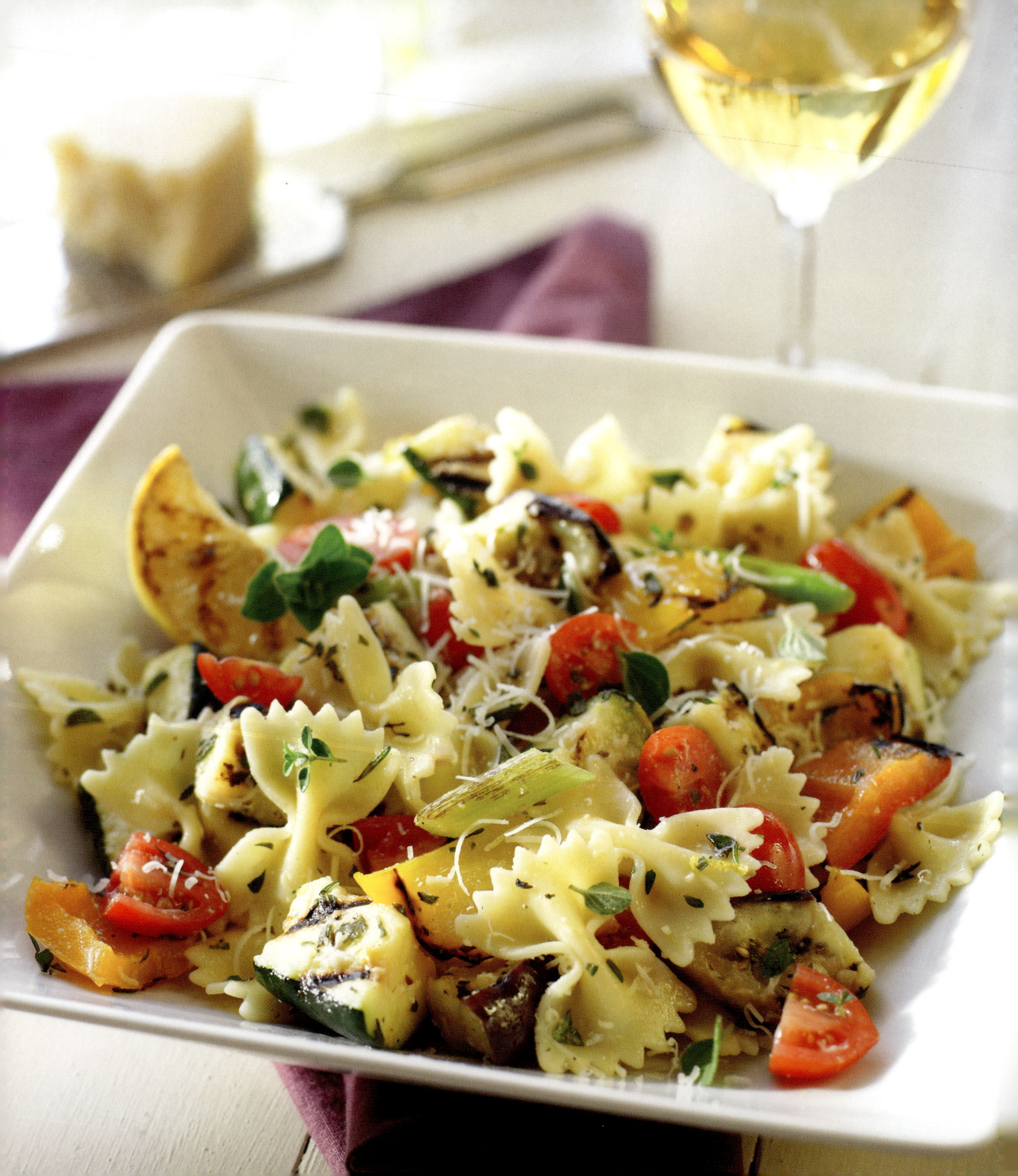

Summer Vegetables with Bowtie Pasta

Grilling brings out the best in summer vegetables, so why not make them the star of the dinner table? Toss them with pasta and plenty of fresh herbs for a satisfying meatless entrée.

- 1 cup fresh herbs, coarsely chopped (basil, oregano, rosemary, parsley)
- 3 tablespoons extra virgin olive oil
- 2 teaspoons grated lemon peel
- 1 clove garlic, minced
- Salt and pepper to taste
- 1 small eggplant, peeled, if desired, and sliced 1/2 inch thick
- 2 medium zucchini, halved lengthwise
- 1 bell pepper, quartered and seeded
- 1 bunch green onion, trimmed
- 1 small lemon, halved
- 12 ounces bowtie pasta (about 6 cups), cooked according to package directions
- 3/4 cup chopped tomato
- 2 ounces (1/2 cup) grated parmesan cheese

In small bowl, combine herbs, olive oil, lemon peel, garlic, salt, and pepper.

Brush eggplant, zucchini, and bell pepper with herb mixture. Place vegetables on grid over medium-high heat; grill until crisp-tender and lightly charred, about 3 to 5 minutes per side. Brush green onions with herb mixture. Place onions diagonally on grid over medium-high heat; grill turning occasionally until crisp-tender and lightly charred, about 3 to 5 minutes. Brush cut-sides of lemon with herb mixture. Place lemons cut-side down on oiled grid over medium-high heat; grill until lightly charred and grill marks appear, about 2 to 3 minutes. Cut grilled vegetables into bite-size pieces.

In large bowl, combine grilled vegetables, pasta, tomato, and cheese. Squeeze lemon halves over pasta and drizzle remaining herb mixture over top; toss until well mixed. Serve warm or chilled.

Makes 6-8 servings

GREG'S GRILLING TIP *A jellyroll pan or baking sheet with sides makes it easy to carry lots of food to and from the grill. If you have raw meat on the tray, be sure to wash it thoroughly before you bring cooked food inside.*

technique savvy

Veggies in a Basket

Love grilled vegetables but hate the ones that get away and fall through the grate? A grill basket is your best friend!

Some are shaped like a bowl with holes. Brush the inside of the basket with a little olive oil to prevent sticking. Cut veggies in similar-size pieces, and toss with oil and seasonings. Place the basket on the grid and add the veggies that need the most cooking time. Cover and grill stirring occasionally. Add quick-cooking veggies as you go until everything is crisp-tender.

If you prefer a long-handled wire basket that opens like a book, oil the basket and add the seasoned veggies. Place it on the fire, shaking and turning occasionally.

Whichever style you choose, this is one grilling gadget you can't live without!

Per serving

Calories 267
Fat 8 g
Cholesterol 4 mg
Sodium 91 mg
Carbohydrate 42 g
Fiber 6 g

Smoky Grilled Quesadillas

These easy, cheesy quesadillas with all the trimmings make a terrific meatless entrée. Assemble the quesadillas early in the day, then stash them in the refrigerator until you fire up the grill.

2 teaspoons olive oil
¼ cup minced onion
2 cloves garlic, minced
1 can (15 ounces) black beans, rinsed, drained, and coarsely puréed
⅓ cup water
1 teaspoon ground cumin
Salt and pepper to taste
8 flour tortillas (8-inch diameter)
1 package (8 ounces) shredded monterey jack cheese (about 2 cups)
1 can (4.5 ounces) chopped green chiles, drained
Shredded iceberg lettuce, diced tomato, salsa, dairy sour cream, guacamole

In medium skillet, heat olive oil over medium-high heat. Add onion and garlic; cook stirring frequently until onion wilts. Add beans, water, cumin, salt, and pepper; cook stirring frequently until heated through. (Mixture should be thick but spreadable.)

Spread bean mixture over 4 of the tortillas; top with cheese and green chiles. Place remaining tortillas on top of filling.

Place quesadillas on oiled grid over medium-high heat; grill until cheese is melted and tortillas are crisp, about 2 to 3 minutes per side. Cut quesadillas into wedges. Serve immediately with desired toppings.

Makes 6-8 servings

GREG'S GRILLING TIP
The easiest way to clean the grate is to heat it up and clean it with a long-handled wire brush. Another good tool is just a piece of wadded-up foil with a pair of tongs. The foil just gets tossed in the trash after use.

---

cuisine savvy
Thanks, Henry!

Those of us who love the flavor of charcoal grilling can thank Henry Ford. Yes, *that* Henry Ford. The famous "Woody" station wagon bodies he mass-produced in the 1920's left behind a lot of unused scraps. Not one to let anything go to waste, Ford had a chemical plant constructed as part of his manufacturing complex to recycle wood scraps into all sorts of by-products.

Thus from sawdust and wood was born the charcoal briquette. With the help of his business partner, these handy briquettes went into commercial production soon after and began a new chapter in America's barbecue history.

Per serving

Calories 291
Fat 11 g
Cholesterol 25 mg
Sodium 466 mg
Carbohydrate 33 g
Fiber 5 g

Rosemary Garlic Bread

Garlic bread goes "uptown" with a sprinkle of fragrant rosemary and sharp parmesan cheese. It's fabulous with grilled steak, pork, chicken, or fish.

1 loaf (8 ounces) Dierbergs bakery baguette
¼ cup extra virgin olive oil
1 to 2 cloves garlic, minced
½ cup grated parmesan or asiago cheese
2 teaspoons snipped fresh rosemary
½ teaspoon coarse salt

Cut baguette in half crosswise; split each piece horizontally cutting almost but not all the way through. In small bowl, stir together olive oil and garlic. Brush over cut surfaces of bread. In small bowl, combine parmesan and rosemary; sprinkle evenly over bread. Close bread; cut into 1½-inch-thick slices. Reassemble loaf on large sheet of heavy-duty foil. Lightly brush top with water; sprinkle salt over top. Bring sides of foil to center in series of locked folds; fold up ends to seal completely. Place bread on grid over medium indirect heat (see *Indirect-Heat Grilling* on page 7); grill turning every 3 minutes until heated through, about 10 to 15 minutes.

Makes 16 servings

Per serving

Calories 81
Fat 5 g
Cholesterol 2 mg
Sodium 180 mg
Carbohydrate 8 g
Fiber <1 g

Grilled Bruschetta

We've fallen in love with these classic Italian grilled bread rounds. They're perfect as is or topped with our Fresh Tomato Salsa (recipe on page 62).

3 cloves garlic, peeled
½ teaspoon coarse salt
⅓ cup olive oil
1 loaf (8 ounces) Dierbergs bakery sourdough baguette, cut into ¾-inch-thick slices

Using sharp knife, mince garlic; sprinkle with salt while mashing to make a paste. In small bowl, stir together garlic paste and olive oil. Brush lightly over both sides of bread slices. Discard any remaining oil.

Working in batches, place bread slices on oiled grid over medium-high heat; grill until lightly toasted and grill marks appear, about 1 to 2 minutes per side.

Makes abut 24 slices

Per serving

Calories 53
Fat 3 g
Cholesterol 0 mg
Sodium 97 mg
Carbohydrate 5 g
Fiber <1 g

Blushing Sangria

Blushing Sangria

Sip this colorful wine punch with spicy barbecue. It's like a party in a pitcher!

- 1 bottle (750 ml) White Zinfandel
- 1 can (11.5 ounces) white grape juice concentrate (undiluted)
- 1 cup peach- or berry-flavored vodka
- 1 lime, thinly sliced
- 1 peach, sliced
- 1 kiwi, peeled and sliced
- 1 cup fresh blackberries or raspberries
- 6 fresh strawberries, halved

In large clear pitcher, combine White Zinfandel, grape juice concentrate, vodka, and lime; stir briskly to combine. Chill several hours or overnight. About 30 minutes before serving, add peach, kiwi, and berries. Serve over ice.

Makes 6 servings

TIP For frozen slushies, omit lime, peach, kiwi, and berries. Place Sangria in 2-quart freezer container. Cover and freeze until solid. Scoop into glasses. Garnish with fruit.

Per serving

Calories 339
Fat 0 g
Cholesterol 0 mg
Sodium 19 mg
Carbohydrate 41 g
Fiber 0 g

Paradise Coolers

Can't get away this summer? Escape to your patio instead. One sip of this cool and fruity punch will remind you of a tropical vacation.

- 1 can (12 ounces) frozen pineapple-orange juice concentrate, thawed (undiluted)
- 1 bottle (1 liter) mango or other tropical-flavored sparkling water
- 1 cup light rum
- 1 cup coconut-flavored rum
- ¼ cup fresh lime juice
- Orange or lime slices

In large clear pitcher, combine all ingredients except citrus slices; stir briskly to combine. Chill several hours or overnight. Serve over ice. Garnish with fresh orange or lime slice.

Makes 8 servings

TIP For a family-friendly drink, omit rum and add 1 cup water plus 1 teaspoon coconut extract.

Per serving

Calories 222
Fat 0 g
Cholesterol 0 mg
Sodium 20 mg
Carbohydrate 29 g
Fiber 0 g

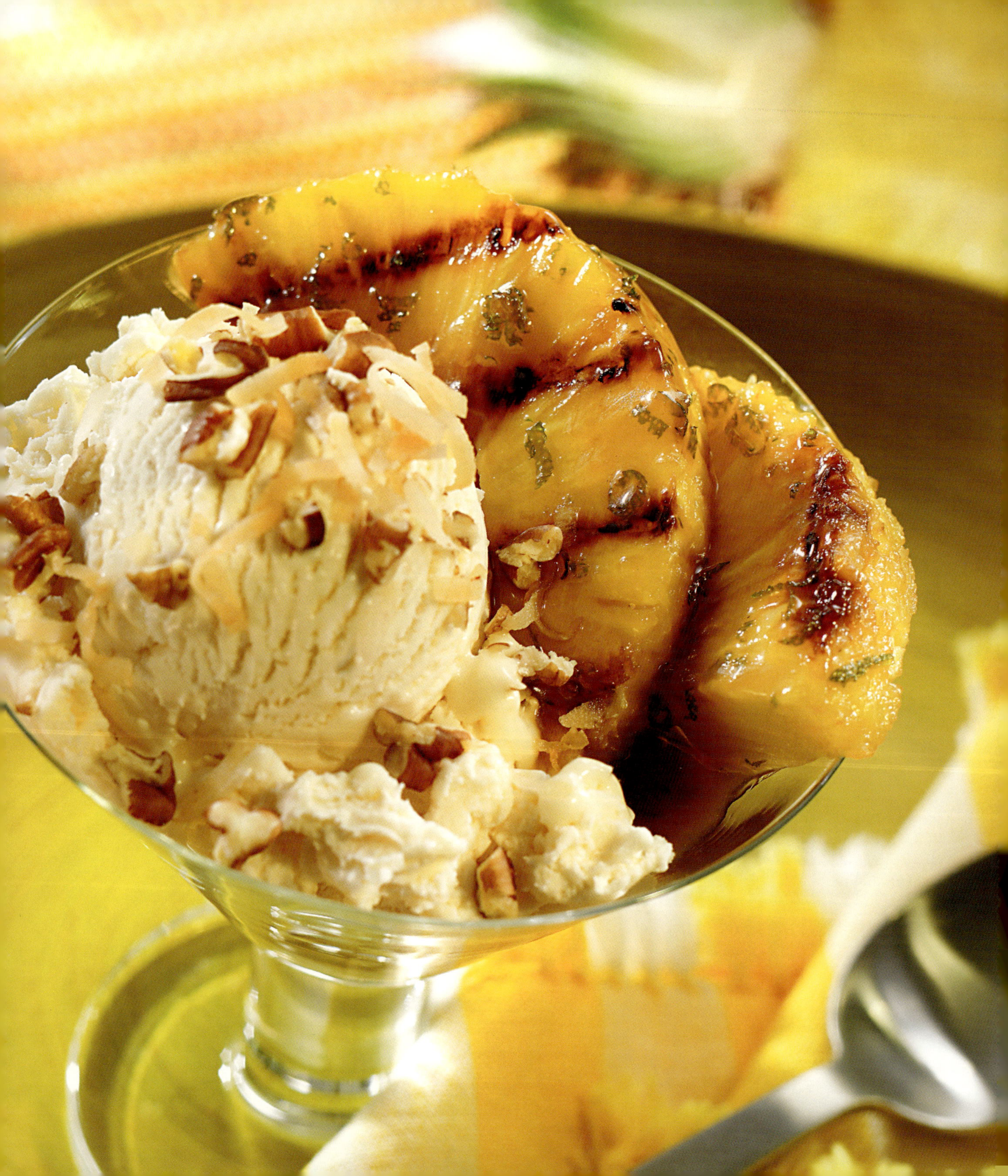

desserts

Grilled Pineapple Sundaes	84
Glazed Grilled Bananas	84
Mojito Ribbon Cake	85
Classic Strawberry Shortcake	86
Blackberry Shortcakes with Lemon Cream	87
Berry Peachy Cobbler	87
Berry Patriotic Pie	88
Pink Lemonade Ice Cream Delight	88
Heavenly Hash Ice Box Cake	90

◀ *Grilled Pineapple Sundaes*
Recipe on page 84

Grilled Pineapple Sundaes

Grilled fruit? You bet! Grill fresh pineapple slices dipped in caramel sauce. Then top them with vanilla ice cream, crunchy pecans, and toasted coconut for a decadent dessert.

Per serving with 1/2 cup ice cream

Calories 330
Fat 18 g
Cholesterol 42 mg
Sodium 122 mg
Carbohydrate 39 g
Fiber 2 g

- 1 fresh pineapple, peeled and cored
- 1/3 cup chopped pecans
- 1/3 cup sweetened flaked coconut
- 2 tablespoons butter
- 1/4 cup firmly packed brown sugar
- 2 tablespoons dark rum or lime juice
- 1 teaspoon grated lime peel
- 1 teaspoon vanilla extract
- 1/8 teaspoon salt
- Vanilla ice cream

Cut pineapple into 6 rings; set aside. In small skillet, combine pecans and coconut over medium heat; cook stirring frequently until fragrant and lightly toasted, about 3 minutes. Remove from skillet; set aside to cool.

In same skillet, melt butter over medium heat. Add brown sugar, rum, lime peel, vanilla, and salt; stir until brown sugar is melted. Dip pineapple slices in mixture, coating both sides. Place slices on oiled grid over medium-low heat; grill until slices are lightly caramelized and heated through, about 2 minutes per side. Place grilled pineapple slices on serving plates. Top each with scoop of ice cream; sprinkle pecan mixture over top. Drizzle remaining sauce over pineapple. Serve immediately.

Makes 6 servings

Glazed Grilled Bananas

Substitute light or dark rum for the spiced rum, or use 1/2 cup orange juice instead. Any way you try it, it's simply fabulous!

Per serving with 1/2 cup ice cream

Calories 339
Fat 18 g
Cholesterol 48 mg
Sodium 62 mg
Carbohydrate 39 g
Fiber 2 g

- 3 tablespoons butter
- 1/4 cup fresh orange juice
- 1/4 cup spiced dark rum
- 3 tablespoons brown sugar
- 1 teaspoon ground cinnamon
- 1/4 teaspoon ground allspice
- 3 firm bananas
- Vanilla ice cream
- 1/4 cup chopped walnuts or pecans, toasted

In small skillet, melt butter over medium heat. Add orange juice, rum, brown sugar, cinnamon, and allspice; cook stirring frequently until brown sugar melts and glaze is bubbly.

Cut unpeeled bananas in half lengthwise; brush cut-sides with some of the glaze. Place bananas cut-side up on grid over medium-high heat; cover and grill until peels are lightly charred and fruit begins to come away from peel, about 4 minutes.

Place grilled banana halves on serving plates. Top each with scoop of ice cream; sprinkle walnuts over top. Drizzle remaining glaze over ice cream. Serve immediately.

Makes 6 servings

Mojito Ribbon Cake

We've captured the flavors of this popular Cuban cocktail in a light and luscious cake. It's a cool finale to a meal from the grill, and it freezes beautifully for make-ahead convenience.

1 box (18.25 ounces) yellow cake mix with pudding
2 teaspoons grated lime peel
1/3 cup light rum
1 cup fresh mint leaves
1/2 cup sugar
1/2 cup water
2 tablespoons fresh lime juice
2 cups heavy whipping cream
1 cup sliced almonds, toasted (optional)
Fresh mint

Lightly coat 11 x 15-inch jellyroll pan with no-stick cooking spray. Line bottom of pan with parchment and lightly coat with cooking spray; set aside.

Prepare cake mix according to package directions, adding lime peel to batter. Pour batter into prepared pan. Bake in 350°F. oven until wooden pick inserted in center comes out clean, about 12 to 14 minutes. Cool in pan for 10 minutes. Turn cake out onto waxed paper; remove parchment paper. Use wooden skewer to poke deep holes into warm cake. **1** Brush rum over warm cake; cool completely. Cut cooled cake into three 5 x 11-inch sections.

Meanwhile, in small saucepan, combine mint and sugar. Using muddler or back of wooden spoon, mash mint leaves with sugar until leaves are bruised (see *Step-by-Step Instructions* on page 70). Stir in water; bring to a boil stirring occasionally over medium-high heat. Reduce heat and simmer without stirring for 5 minutes. Remove from heat and steep for 10 minutes; strain. Stir in lime juice. Cover and chill.

In large chilled mixer bowl, beat whipping cream at medium speed while slowing adding mint syrup until well blended. Beat at high speed until stiff peaks form.

Place 1 section of cake, rum-side up, onto serving plate; **2** spread about 3/4 cup of the whipped cream over top. Repeat procedure with remaining 2 cake layers and whipped cream. Chill cake and remaining whipped cream for several hours or overnight.

To serve, slice cake and place on serving plates. Top with dollop of whipped cream. **3** If desired, sprinkle with nuts and garnish with fresh mint.

Makes 10-12 servings

technique savvy

Step-by-Step Instructions

Per serving

Calories 425
Fat 26 g
Cholesterol 108 mg
Sodium 323 mg
Carbohydrate 45 g
Fiber 0 g

Classic Strawberry Shortcake

These rich, tender biscuits are a snap to make in the food processor. Avoid overhandling the dough which can make them tough.

technique savvy

Grilled Shortcakes

No time to make shortcakes? Here's a quick and easy substitute. Cut a purchased angel food cake into 3/4-inch-thick slices or a purchased pound cake into 1/2-inch-thick slices. Place slices cut-side down on clean grid over low heat and grill for 1 to 2 minutes per side or until toasted. Serve toasted cake slices with fresh fruit and whipped cream for an easy dessert.

SHORTCAKES
- 2 cups flour
- 3 tablespoons granulated sugar
- 1 tablespoon baking powder
- 1/4 teaspoon salt
- 4 tablespoons butter, chilled and cut into pieces
- 2 tablespoons solid shortening, chilled and cut into pieces
- 1/3 cup milk
- 1 egg
- 1 teaspoon vanilla extract
- 2 teaspoons granulated or raw sugar

TOPPING
- 3 cups sliced fresh strawberries
- 2 to 3 tablespoons granulated sugar
- 1 cup heavy whipping cream
- 2 tablespoons powdered sugar
- 8 whole fresh strawberries (optional)
- Fresh mint (optional)

FOR SHORTCAKES In work bowl of food processor fitted with steel knife blade, combine flour, the 3 tablespoons granulated sugar, baking powder, and salt; pulse to blend. Add butter and shortening; pulse until mixture resembles coarse meal. In small bowl, whisk together milk, egg, and vanilla. Pour milk mixture over crumbs; pulse just until soft dough forms. Turn dough out onto lightly floured surface. Divide dough into 8 equal portions. Gently roll each portion into ball; place on parchment-lined baking sheet and flatten to about 3/4 inch thick. Sprinkle the 2 teaspoons sugar over tops of shortcakes. Bake in 375°F. oven until golden brown, about 15 minutes.

FOR TOPPING In medium bowl, combine strawberries and the granulated sugar. Let stand 30 minutes, or cover and chill up to 2 hours.

In large chilled mixer bowl, beat whipping cream and the powdered sugar at low speed until well blended. Beat at high speed until stiff peaks form. Chill until ready to serve.

TO ASSEMBLE Split shortcakes horizontally. Place bottoms on individual serving plates. Top with sweetened berries, dollop of whipped cream, and shortcake tops. If desired, garnish with whole strawberry and mint.

Makes 8 servings

Per serving

Calories 374
Fat 22 g
Cholesterol 85 mg
Sodium 189 mg
Carbohydrate 40 g
Fiber 2 g

Blackberry Shortcakes with Lemon Cream

The combination of plump, juicy blackberries and cool, lemony whipped cream is heavenly. Look for lemon curd in the jam and jelly aisle.

3 cups fresh blackberries
2 to 3 tablespoons sugar
2 tablespoons raspberry-flavored liqueur (Chambord) (optional)
1 cup heavy whipping cream
1/2 cup lemon curd
8 Classic Shortcakes (recipe on page 86), OR 8 slices grilled angel food or pound cake (see *Grilled Shortcakes* on page 86)
Fresh mint (optional)

Reserve 8 blackberries for garnish. Combine remaining blackberries, sugar, and liqueur in large bowl. If desired, lightly crush berries. Let stand 30 minutes, or cover and chill for up to 2 hours.

In large chilled mixer bowl, beat whipping cream and lemon curd at low speed until well blended. Beat at high speed until stiff peaks form. Chill until ready to serve.

Split shortcakes horizontally. Place bottoms on individual serving plates. Top with sweetened berries, dollop of lemon cream, and shortcake tops. If desired, garnish with whole berry and mint.

Makes 8 servings

Per serving

Calories 460
Fat 31 g
Cholesterol 90 mg
Sodium 204 mg
Carbohydrate 59 g
Fiber 4 g

Berry Peachy Cobbler

Nothing says summer like a warm, bubbly cobbler bursting with fresh fruit. Chop up a refrigerated pie crust and toss it with sugar and cinnamon for the easiest topping ever!

5 cups peeled and cubed ripe peaches (about 8 medium)
1 cup fresh raspberries
1/2 to 3/4 cup sugar
2 tablespoons cornstarch
2 teaspoons ground cinnamon (divided)
2 tablespoons sugar
1 refrigerated pie crust (1/2 of 15-ounce package), cut into 1/2-inch pieces
Vanilla ice cream (optional)

Lightly coat 7 x 11-inch baking dish with no-stick cooking spray. Add peaches and raspberries. In small bowl, stir together the 1/2 cup sugar, cornstarch, and 1 teaspoon of the cinnamon. (If fruit is tart, add up to 1/4 cup additional sugar.) Sprinkle over fruit; gently toss until well mixed.

In medium bowl, combine the 2 tablespoons sugar and remaining 1 teaspoon cinnamon. Add pie crust pieces; toss until well mixed. Sprinkle evenly over peaches. Bake in 350°F. oven until top is brown and juices bubble in center, about 20 to 25 minutes. Serve warm with vanilla ice cream, if desired.

Makes 8 servings

Per serving

Calories 361
Fat 8 g
Cholesterol 5 mg
Sodium 111 mg
Carbohydrate 73 g
Fiber 8 g

Berry Patriotic Pie

Don't wait for a summer holiday to enjoy this all-American pie. A fluffy cream cheese filling topped with a medley of tart, tangy berries will make you a dessert hero!

Per serving

Calories 362
Fat 24 g
Cholesterol 68 mg
Sodium 291 mg
Carbohydrate 31 g
Fiber 3 g

1 1/4 cups graham cracker crumbs
2 tablespoons granulated sugar
5 tablespoons butter, melted
1 package (8 ounces) cream cheese (not light or fat-free)
1/2 cup powdered sugar
1 teaspoon vanilla extract
1/2 teaspoon grated orange peel
1/2 cup heavy whipping cream
3 cups mixed fresh berries (strawberries, raspberries, blueberries, blackberries)
Powdered sugar

In 9-inch pie plate, combine graham cracker crumbs and the granulated sugar; stir in butter. Press onto bottom and up sides of pie plate. Bake in 350°F. oven until lightly browned, about 8 to 10 minutes. Cool completely.

In large mixer bowl, beat cream cheese, the 1/2 cup powdered sugar, vanilla, and orange peel at low speed until smooth. Add whipping cream; beat at medium speed until lightly and fluffy. Spread into cooled crust. Place berries on pie, covering filling completely. Chill at least 3 hours. Dust with powdered sugar before serving.

Makes 8 servings

Pink Lemonade Ice Cream Delight

Lemon desserts are Dierbergs School of Cooking Manager Jennifer Kassel's signature, and this easy finale is one of her favorites. It's cool, refreshing, and the perfect ending to a spicy barbecue meal!

Per serving

Calories 284
Fat 15 g
Cholesterol 34 mg
Sodium 111 mg
Carbohydrate 35 g
Fiber 1 g

2 cups shortbread cookie crumbs
1/4 cup butter, melted
1/2 gallon vanilla ice cream
1 can (12 ounces) frozen pink lemonade concentrate, thawed (undiluted)
1 tablespoon grated lemon peel
1 container (12 ounces) frozen whipped topping, thawed

In small bowl, stir together cookie crumbs and butter. Reserve 1/4 cup of the mixture for garnish. Press remaining crumbs onto bottom of 9 x 13-inch metal baking pan. Bake in 350°F. oven until lightly browned, about 8 to 10 minutes. Cool completely.

In large mixing bowl, combine ice cream, lemonade, and lemon peel; let stand 10 to 15 minutes to soften. Stir until well blended. Fold in whipped topping. Spread over cooled crust. Cover and freeze for several hours or overnight. Cut into squares. Garnish each square with reserved crumb mixture.

Makes 16-20 servings

Berry Patriotic Pie

Heavenly Hash Ice Box Cake

A taste of nostalgia! Soft and fluffy marshmallows are the perfect complement to crunchy bits of chocolate and almond.

cuisine savvy

Ice Box Cakes

Popularized in the 1920's, ice box cakes are really more concept than recipe, transforming prepared ingredients into luscious desserts – no baking necessary. Just stir together cookies or cake cubes with pudding and whipped cream, press into a pan and chill overnight. You'll have a delicious ice box cake with hardly any effort.

In the 1930's and 40's, electric refrigerators replaced old-fashioned ice boxes and savvy cooks began calling them refrigerator cakes. Whichever name you prefer, these old fashioned desserts are still just as easy and delicious as they were generations ago.

1 angel food cake (16 ounces), cut into 1-inch cubes
1 bag (10.5 ounces) miniature marshmallows
1 jar (7 ounces) marshmallow créme
½ cup milk
1 bag (12 ounces) semisweet chocolate chips
½ teaspoon almond extract
1 bottle (7.25 ounces) chocolate-flavored hard-shell topping
¼ cup sliced almonds, toasted

Lightly coat 9 x 13-inch baking dish with no-stick cooking spray; set aside.

In large mixing bowl, combine cake cubes and miniature marshmallows; toss to mix. In large microwave-safe bowl, combine marshmallow créme and milk. Microwave (high) for 2 minutes. Add chocolate chips. Stir until chocolate is melted and smooth. Stir in almond extract. Working quickly, drizzle chocolate mixture over cake mixture; toss to coat all pieces. Press half of cake mixture into prepared dish with spatula. Drizzle half of the ice cream topping over top. Repeat procedure. Sprinkle almonds over top. Chill for 3 to 4 hours. Cut into 3-inch squares.

Makes 12 servings

Per serving

Calories 485
Fat 17 g
Cholesterol 1 mg
Sodium 335 mg
Carbohydrate 83 g
Fiber 2 g

Nutrition Information

In *Grilling*, you'll find heart-healthy recipes identified by the red heart ♥ logo shown with the nutrition analysis. Dierbergs Markets along with Missouri Baptist Medical Center, a member of BJC HealthCare, proudly sponsor *Eat Hearty*®, an informational program aimed at helping you choose a heart-healthy eating plan.

Criteria Used for Calculating Nutrition Information

- Whenever a choice is given, the following are used: The first ingredient; the lesser amount of an ingredient; the larger number of servings.

- Ingredients without specific amounts listed, such as "optional" or "toppings," have not been included in the analysis.

- The nutrition information provided in *Grilling* was calculated using *Nutritionist Pro*, a nutrition analysis program developed by First DataBank, Inc. for the Hearst Corporation. The information is believed to be reliable and correct.

- The nutrition professionals compiling the information have made every effort to present the most accurate information available, but have undertaken no independent examination, investigation or verification of information provided by original sources. Therefore, Dierbergs assumes no liability and denies any responsibility for incorrect information resulting from the use of the nutrition information provided in *Grilling*.

Ingredients Used in Nutrition Calculation

- Certain ingredients are considered "standard" for nutrition analysis. They include large eggs, 2% milk, lean ground beef, and canned broth. Other ingredient selections were based on information from the USDA and/or readily available brands.

- If a recipe specifies reduced-fat/reduced-sodium products in the ingredient list, these products were used for nutrition analysis.

- Some recipes meet *Eat Hearty* criteria without modification. You may wish to make additional substitutions to further reduce the fat/sodium content of these recipes.

Recipe Criteria

Recipes that have a red heart ♥ logo in this cookbook must not exceed the following guidelines per serving:

3 g fat/480 mg sodium*

Beverages (alcoholic beverages have not been considered)
Appetizers
Soups served as an appetizer
Vegetable side dishes
Breads and rolls

5 g fat/720 mg sodium*

Meat salads
Starch side dishes
Salads (vegetable/pasta/fruit)
Desserts
Breakfast breads and muffins

10 g fat/960 mg sodium*

Main dishes
Combination entrées (such as spaghetti and meatballs)
Entrée soups
Entrée sandwiches

*Sodium levels are a suggested level only. If you are following a sodium-restricted diet, please consult your physician or dietitian for specific recommendations.

How Much Meat Should I Buy?

As you plan your menu, you want enough to serve everyone comfortably without necessarily having leftovers for days on end. Here's a little help with your shopping list.

In general, plan on 3 to 4 servings per pound of boneless meats, like chicken breasts, ground meats, fish, pork chops, steaks, and roasts.

Bone-in cuts are a little more challenging. Allow for the weight of the bone when determining how much to purchase.

Bone-In	Servings Per Pound
Beef	
Steak	2 to 3
Pork	
Chops	2 to 3
Roast	2 to 3
Poultry	
Cornish Hens	1 to 2
Chicken, whole	2
Turkey Breast	2
Turkey, whole	1
Fish	
Shrimp, in shell	3 to 4

Equivalents

Pinch or dash	= less than 1/8 teaspoon
1 tablespoon	= 3 teaspoons
1 fluid ounce	= 2 tablespoons
1/4 cup	= 4 tablespoons
1/3 cup	= 5 tablespoons + 1 teaspoon
1 cup	= 16 tablespoons, 8 fluid ounces, or 1/2 pint
1 pint	= 2 cups or 16 fluid ounces
1 quart	= 4 cups, 32 fluid ounces, or 2 pints
1 gallon	= 4 quarts or 128 fluid ounces
1 pound	= 16 ounces
1 medium lemon	= 3 tablespoons juice, 2 to 3 teaspoons zest
1 medium lime	= 1 1/2 to 2 tablespoons juice, 1 teaspoon zest
1 medium orange	= 1/3 to 1/2 cup juice, 1 1/2 to 2 tablespoons zest
1 bottle (750 ml) wine	= about 3 1/4 cups (25.4 fluid ounces)
4 ounces cheese	= 1 cup crumbled, grated or shredded

Food Safety

- Thaw frozen food in the refrigerator overnight. Do not thaw food at room temperature.

- To quickly thaw frozen food, place tightly wrapped food in large bowl and add cold water to cover. Change the water every 30 minutes until the food is thawed.

- Raw meat should never sit at room temperature for more than one hour, especially in hot weather.

- After handling raw meat, poultry, or seafood, always wash your hands in hot soapy water.

- Wash platters or plates used to transport raw meat to the grill, or use a different plate for cooked meat to avoid cross-contamination.

- If you plan on serving some of the sauce with the cooked meat, reserve that portion of sauce prior to basting the raw meat. The same is true for marinades. If using part of the marinade as the dressing for salad, reserve some for dressing and use the remainder for marinating the meat.

- Use an instant-read or meat thermometer to determine internal temperatures of meat (see *Minimum Safe Internal Temperature* on page 9).

Dierbergs School of Cooking

Dierbergs School of Cooking Since 1978

Southroads Center
Tesson Ferry and I-270
St. Louis, MO 63128

West Oak Center
Olive Boulevard and
   Craig Road
Creve Coeur, MO 63141

Clarkson/Clayton Center
Clarkson and Clayton Roads
Ellisville, MO 63011

Bogey Hills Plaza
Zumbehl Road and I-70
St. Charles, MO 63303

Edwardsville Crossing
Troy Road and
   Governor's Parkway
Edwardsville, IL 62025

636-812-1336 (Missouri)
618-622-5353 (Illinois)

Explore the world of cooking at Dierbergs, and have a little fun in our kitchen — and yours!

- Choose from dozens of topics from appetizers, entrées, or desserts, to seafood, wines, restaurant specialties, regional cooking styles, ethnic foods, heart-healthy cooking, and much more.
- Classes taught by noted chefs, restaurateurs, cookbook authors, caterers, and staff instructors.
- Custom classes for birthday parties, special events, and corporate team-building events.

For more information on Dierbergs School of Cooking or cooking class schedules:
www.dierbergs.com

For information on Dierbergs cookbooks or magazine subscriptions:
publications@dierbergs.com

Index

BEEF
Balsamic Grilled Sirloin, 24 ♥
Beef and Portabella Burgers, 29 ♥
Burger Basics, 29
Chicago-Style Steaks/Blue Cheese Butter, 20 ♦
Mesquite Smoked Brisket, 28 ♥
Petite Tenders with Greek Herbed Tomato Salad, 24 ♦
Pickapeppa Beef Kabobs, 26 ♥♦
Santa Fe Tostadas/Chipotle Sour Cream, 21
Set Up a Fajita Bar, 23
Steak Fajitas with Pico de Gallo, 23 ♥♦
Steaks, 20

BEVERAGES
Blushing Sangria, 81 ♦
Paradise Coolers, 81

BREADS
Cornmeal Pizza Crust, 50 ♥
Grilled Bruschetta, 79 ♥
Rosemary Garlic Bread, 79

BRINES
Basic Brine, 16
  Whiskey Pepper Chops, 37 ♦
Beer Brine, 16
  Sweet and Spicy Pork Steaks, 30
  Sweet and Spicy Spareribs, 30
Brining, 16
Java Brine, 16
  Java BBQ Chicken, 44 ♥

BUTTERS
Blue Cheese Butter, 20 ♦
Citrus Butter, 59
Compound Butters, 37
Molasses Butter, 37 ♦

CHICKEN
Beer Can Chicken, 43 ♥♦
Caribbean Chicken Kabobs, 26 ♥
Chicken Satay/Pineapple Chutney Glaze, 49 ♦
Chicken with Lemon-Scented Tapenade, 46 ♥
CLT Sandwich, 47 ♥
Hens Under Bricks, 42 ♥♦
How Much Chicken, 46
Java BBQ Chicken, 44 ♥
Mediterranean Chicken Pizza, 50 ♥
Pounding Chicken Breasts, 47
Tropical Spiced Chicken with Ginger Peach Salsa, 44 ♥♦

CONTRIBUTED BY
Sally Bruns, 75
Cathy Chipley, 23
Loretta Evans, 38
Ginger Gall, 42
Karen Hurych, 72
Jennifer Kassel, 88
Therese Lewis, 58
Nancy Lorenz, 20
Chef Jack West MacMurray III, 32
Pam Pahl, 49
Carol Ziemann, 54

CUISINE SAVVY
Ice Box Cakes, 90
Thanks, Henry!, 78
What is Satay?, 49
What is Tandoori?, 15

DESSERTS
Berry Patriotic Pie, 88 ♦
Berry Peachy Cobbler, 87
Blackberry Shortcakes with Lemon Cream, 87
Classic Strawberry Shortcake, 86
Glazed Grilled Bananas, 84
Grilled Pineapple Sundaes, 84 ♦
Grilled Shortcakes, 86
Heavenly Hash Ice Box Cake, 90
Ice Box Cakes, 90
Mojito Ribbon Cake, 85
Pink Lemonade Ice Cream Delight, 88

FISH *See also Seafood*
Balsamic Fish Steaks with Artichoke Aïoli, 58 ♥
Grilling Fish, 59
Grilling Tuna, 56
Herbed Tilapia with Citrus Butter, 59 ♥
Salmon on a Plank, 54 ♥♦
Teriyaki Grilled Salmon, 54
Tuna Salad Niçoise/French Vinaigrette, 56 ♦

FRUITS
Berry Patriotic Pie, 88 ♦
Berry Peachy Cobbler, 87
Blackberry Shortcakes with Lemon Cream, 87
Classic Strawberry Shortcake, 86
Fresh Fruit Salsa, 63 ♥
Ginger Peach Salsa, 63 ♥♦
Glazed Grilled Bananas, 84
Grilled Pineapple Sundaes, 84 ♦
Mango and Lime Slaw, 72 ♥
Mango Bourbon Sauce, 32 ♥♦
Minty Melon Salad, 70 ♥♦
Raspberry Balsamic Pork on Greens, 35 ♥
Strawberry Salsa, 63 ♥
Tropical Fruit Salsa, 63 ♥
Watermelon Salsa, 63 ♥

GLAZES
Caribbean Glaze, 13 ♥
   Caribbean Chicken Kabobs, 26 ♥
Margarita Glaze, 38 ♥
Pickapeppa Glaze, 13 ♥
   Pickapeppa Beef Kabobs, 26 ♥◆
   Tropical Spiced Chicken, 44 ♥◆
Pineapple Chutney Glaze, 49 ♥◆
Raspberry Balsamic Glaze, 13 ♥

INGREDIENT SAVVY
Chipotles in Adobo Sauce, 21
Fresh Asparagus, 75
Fresh Chiles, 63
Fresh Herbs, 67
How Much Chicken, 46
Steaks, 20

KABOBS
Caribbean Chicken Kabobs, 26 ♥
Chicken Satay/Pineapple Chutney Glaze, 49 ◆
Chili Cherry Pork Kabobs, 26
Gingered Shrimp Salad, 53 ♥
Kabob Klues, 26
Mojo Shrimp Salad, 53 ♥◆
Pickapeppa Beef Kabobs, 26 ♥◆
Tuscan Grilled Vegetables, 73 ♥

MARINADES
Balsamic Marinade, 14
   Balsamic Grilled Sirloin, 24 ♥
French Vinaigrette, 56
   Tuna Salad Niçoise/French Vinaigrette, 56 ◆
Ginger Marinade, 14
   Gingered Shrimp Salad, 53 ♥
Mojo Marinade, 14
   Mojo Shrimp Salad, 53 ♥◆
Red Wine Marinade, 15
Safe Marinating is No Accident, 14
Tandoori Marinade, 15
Tuscan Marinade, 15
   Tuscan Grilled Vegetables, 73 ♥

MEATLESS ENTRÉES
Bella on a Bun, 74
Smoky Grilled Quesadillas, 78
Summer Vegetables with Bowtie Pasta, 77 ♥◆

PASTA
Italian Sausage and Pasta Grill, 39
Summer Vegetables with Bowtie Pasta, 77 ♥◆

PIZZA
Cornmeal Pizza Crust, 50 ♥
Mediterranean Chicken Pizza, 50 ♥

PORK
Asian Barbecued Pork Wraps, 34 ♥
Chili Cherry Chops, 38 ♥
Chili Cherry Pork Kabobs, 26
Italian Sausage and Pasta Grill, 39
Maple Mustard Pork Roast, 31 ♥
Margarita Glazed Pork Chops, 38 ♥
Raspberry Balsamic Pork on Greens, 35 ♥
Rubbed Pork Tenderloin with Mango
   Bourbon Sauce, 32 ♥◆
Sweet and Spicy Pork Steaks, 30
Sweet and Spicy Spareribs, 30
Tender Juicy Pork, 35
Whiskey Pepper Chops/Molasses Butter, 37 ◆
Wurst Comes to Wurst, 39

RUBS
Fresh Herb Rub, 17
Island Rub, 17
Rubs, 17
Southwest Rub, 17

SALADS
Asian Slaw, 72 ♥
Crisping Greens, 69
Gingered Shrimp Salad, 53 ♥
Greek Cucumber Salad, 68 ♥
Greek Herbed Tomato Salad, 67 ◆
Grilled Baby Potato and Green Bean Salad, 64
Herbed Tomato Mozzarella Salad, 67 ◆
Mango and Lime Slaw, 72 ♥
Minty Melon Salad, 70 ♥◆
Mojo Shrimp Salad, 53 ♥◆
Raspberry Balsamic Pork on Greens, 35 ♥
Southwest Chopped Salad, 69 ♥
Southwest Potato Salad, 65
Tuna Salad Niçoise/French Vinaigrette, 56 ◆

SALSAS
Fresh Fruit Salsa, 63 ♥
Fresh Tomato Salsa, 62 ♥
Ginger Peach Salsa, 63 ♥◆
   Tropical Spiced Chicken with Ginger
   Peach Salsa, 44 ♥◆
Grilled Corn Salsa, 62 ♥◆
Lemon-Scented Tapenade, 46
Pico de Gallo, 23 ♥◆
Strawberry Salsa, 63 ♥
Tropical Fruit Salsa, 63 ♥
Watermelon Salsa, 63 ♥

SANDWICHES/WRAPS
Asian Barbecued Pork Wraps, 34 ♥
Beef and Portabella Burgers, 29 ♥
Bella on a Bun, 74
Burger Basics, 29
CLT Sandwich, 47 ♥
Santa Fe Tostadas with Chipotle
   Sour Cream, 21
Set Up a Fajita Bar, 23
Smoky Grilled Quesadillas, 78
Steak Fajitas with Pico de Gallo, 23 ♥◆

SAUCES
Artichoke Aïoli, 58 ♥
Best-Ever Barbecue Sauce, 12 ♥
    Sweet and Spicy Pork Steaks, 30
    Sweet and Spicy Spareribs, 30
Bring on the Sauce, 12
Chili Cherry Sauce, 12 ♥
    Bacon-Wrapped Turkey Medallions, 51 ♥
    Chili Cherry Chops, 38 ♥
    Chili Cherry Pork Kabobs, 26
Chipotle Sour Cream, 21
Mango Bourbon Sauce, 32 ♥◆
Sassy Cider Sauce, 31 ♥

SEAFOOD *See also Fish*
Gingered Shrimp Salad, 53 ♥
Mojo Shrimp Salad, 53 ♥◆

TECHNIQUE SAVVY
Bring on the Sauce, 12
Brining, 16
Burger Basics, 29
Compound Butters, 37
Covering the Grill, 50
Crisping Greens, 69
Cucumbers, 68
Different Smokes for Different Folks, 31
Fire Temperatures, 38
Foiled Again!, 64
Grill Safety, 8
Grilled Shortcakes, 86
Grilling Fish, 59
Grilling Tuna, 56
Grilling Vegetables, 73
Kabob Klues, 26
Out of Gas, 58
Plank Cooking, 7
Pounding Chicken Breasts, 47
Rubs, 17
Safe Marinating Is No Accident, 14
Safety First, 13
Set Up a Fajita Bar, 23
Standing Time, 9
Tender Juicy Pork, 35
Veggies in a Basket, 77
Weather or Not, 34
Where There's Smoke, 28
Wurst Comes to Wurst, 39

TURKEY
Apricot-Glazed Turkey Tenderloins, 51 ♥
Bacon-Wrapped Turkey Medallions, 51 ♥

VEGETABLES
Grilled Vegetable Time Table, 73
Grilling Vegetables, 73
Veggies in a Basket, 77

Asparagus
Asparagus with Lemon Dijon Sauce, 75
Fresh Asparagus, 75

Corn-on-the-Cob
Grilled Corn Salsa, 62 ♥◆
Southwest Chopped Salad, 69 ♥
Southwest Potato Salad, 65

Green Beans
Grilled Baby Potato and Green Bean Salad, 64
Tuna Salad Niçoise with French Vinaigrette, 56 ◆

Mushrooms
Beef and Portabella Burgers, 29 ♥
Bella on a Bun, 74
Tuscan Grilled Vegetables, 73 ♥

Potatoes
Grilled Baby Potato and Green Bean Salad, 64
Southwest Potato Salad, 65

Tomatoes
Fresh Tomato Salsa, 62 ♥
Greek Herbed Tomato Salad, 67 ◆
    Petite Tenders with Greek Herbed Tomato Salad, 24 ◆
Herbed Tomato Mozzarella Salad, 67 ◆
Mediterranean Chicken Pizza, 50 ♥
Pico de Gallo, 23 ♥◆

Zucchini/Summer Squash
Caribbean Chicken Kabobs, 26 ♥
Chili Cherry Pork Kabobs, 26
Italian Sausage and Pasta Grill, 39
Pickapeppa Beef Kabobs, 26 ♥◆
Summer Vegetables with Bowtie Pasta, 77 ♥◆
Tuscan Grilled Vegetables, 73 ♥

◆ Photograph of Recipe
♥ Heart Healthy Recipe
Items in italic are sidebars